The Ethical Chain

Embedding Morality in Blockchain Systems

Maximillion Smart

Glossary of Key Terms

Blockchain: A decentralized, distributed ledger technology that records transactions in a verifiable and immutable way.

DeFi (Decentralized Finance): A blockchain-based ecosystem that replicates traditional financial services without centralized intermediaries.

DAO (Decentralized Autonomous Organization): An on-chain organization governed by code and token-based voting rather than centralized leadership.

Tokenomics: The design and economics of a token, including supply, distribution, incentives, and governance rights.

Smart Contract: A self-executing program on a blockchain that automatically enforces rules and outcomes when predefined conditions are met.

KYC/AML (Know Your Customer / Anti-Money Laundering): Regulatory frameworks requiring identity verification and monitoring of financial transactions to prevent illicit activities.

Quadratic Voting: A governance method that reduces the influence of large stakeholders by making each additional vote exponentially more expensive.

Zero-Knowledge Proof (ZKP): A cryptographic technique that allows one party to prove a statement is true without revealing any underlying data.

Tokenized Real Estate: The representation of real property interests in digital tokens that can be traded or governed via blockchain.

Ethical Wind-Down: A structured and transparent exit or closure of a protocol, ensuring users are informed, protected, and fairly treated.

Introduction

The Code of Our New World

Blockchain did not appear by accident. It emerged from the ashes of broken promises—collapsing banks, failed governments, and digital systems that promised liberation but delivered surveillance. Its architects were rebels and dreamers, mathematicians and outcasts, all united by a simple conviction: **If you can't trust the institutions, trust the math.**

But as with every great revolution, the questions it raises are more profound than the ones it solves. What began as a technical experiment is now a global operating system, reshaping money, property, identity, and governance. Billions of dollars, lives, and hopes now move across chains that never sleep. The ledger is no longer just a tool; it is the nervous system of a new civilization.

Yet at this crossroads, the world is unprepared.

Politicians argue at the edges, legislating fear as much as foresight. Developers ship code at the speed of imagination, often blind to the social contract their lines of logic will enforce. Ordinary people are caught between euphoria and anxiety, promised empowerment but exposed to unprecedented risk.

This book is written for all of them; for all of us.

What's at Stake

Blockchain technology is not simply digitizing the world as we know it. It is **reprogramming the rules of participation, ownership,** and **belonging**. If the last century's battles were fought over territory, ideology, and capital, the coming century's will be over the invisible: **trust, data,** and **the power to define what is fair.**

- Who decides what counts as money, property, or identity?
- Who holds power when code becomes law, and who is left out?
- How do we ensure that transparency does not become

surveillance, or that access does not become a new form of exploitation?
- What does justice look like when the judge is an algorithm?

These are not distant, academic questions. They are the ground beneath our feet, shifting as we speak. The next 10 years will decide not just who wins in the blockchain era, but what kind of world we will build for generations to come.

A Blueprint and a Warning

This book is not a technical manual. It is a **call to consciousness**; a framework for ethical action, institutional design, and collective imagination. It draws on real stories: projects that have succeeded and failed, communities that have risen and fallen, and laws that have protected and betrayed. It weaves together insights from programmers, policymakers, activists, investors, and citizens from every corner of the globe.

But most of all, it is a warning: **Without ethics, blockchain will repeat the worst mistakes of the systems it seeks to replace, at digital speed and global scale.** The myth of "neutral code" is just that—a myth. Every protocol encodes a philosophy. Every DAO is a new kind of polity. Every token is a bet on what—and who—matters.

An Invitation to Leadership

The chapters that follow are a journey from the origins of decentralized trust, through the trenches of tokenomics and governance, to the frontiers of privacy, regulation, failure, and global convergence. Each chapter challenges you, not just to learn, but to lead. To think beyond profit, beyond hype, beyond technical cleverness—to the deep work of building a world where **technology is the servant of humanity, not its master.**

Whether you are a regulator facing the unknown, a developer chasing the next breakthrough, or a citizen seeking agency in the digital age, this book is your map—and your mirror. It asks only that you bring an open mind and a willingness to ask the hardest questions.

The Real Revolution

The true revolution of blockchain is not technical, but ethical. Not in the code, but in the **choices we make together** to share power, to protect the vulnerable, to remember that trust cannot be automated without conscience.

This is the code of our new world. Let's write it together, wisely, and for all.

Welcome to the next chapter of civilization. Let's make it one worth living in.

Contents

Chapter 1: The Fork in the Code: Why Ethics Must Precede Innovation

Summary:

In every generation, there is a moment when technology outpaces philosophy. A point when what 'we can do' outstrips what 'we have agreed we should do.' Blockchain is that moment for us.

The global financial system is undergoing a silent revolution. Currencies are programmable. Property is fractionalized. Agreements are enforced not by courts, but by code. Power has not merely shifted—it has **disintermediated**. And in this new terrain, there is one thing conspicuously missing:

An ethical framework.

Not a regulatory rulebook.
Not a user agreement.
But a **shared moral architecture**—one designed not to restrict innovation, but to ensure its survivability.

This book exists because that framework does not.

The Illusion of Neutral Code

There is a dangerous myth embedded in the culture of decentralization: if code is open, if protocols are permissionless, then the system is neutral. But neutrality is not what defines a system; outcomes do.

Consider the following:

In 2020, a protocol allowed users to deposit collateral and borrow synthetic assets through a smart contract. A clever user discovered that the price oracle used to determine collateral value lagged by several seconds. In that delay, the user borrowed millions against temporarily inflated collateral, then exited before the price corrected, draining liquidity and leaving other users insolvent.

No law was broken. No security was breached. The exploit simply **existed**

within the rules of the code. Yet the ethical failure is evident: a system was designed with no protection for the community it claimed to empower.

This is what happens when logic is prioritized over impact, when scale overtakes caution, when code is law. But law? It has no conscience.

A New System Demands New Foundations

In traditional finance, trust is derived from structure—FDIC guarantees, legal arbitration, and fiduciary duty. These elements are far from perfect, but they are designed to prevent collapse, mitigate abuse, and offer redress.

In decentralized finance (DeFi) and tokenized economies, those institutions have been replaced by smart contracts and DAOs. The benefits are clear: transparency, automation, and access. But the losses are profound:

- No regulator to halt market manipulation.
- No court to unwind unjust liquidations.
- No intermediary to explain risk or stop predation.

And so, the question arises: If decentralization removes the referee, who protects the game?

The answer must be: We do. Through design. Through governance. Through ethics.

What This Book Proposes

This book is not a technology manual. It is not an investment thesis. It is a foundation—a principled infrastructure for a decentralized world. It offers no speculation, no evangelism, no utopian promise.

Instead, it offers a challenge to every protocol, platform, investor, and regulator—**build systems worthy of the trust they require.**

To do that, we must:

- Reconstruct trust without intermediaries.
- Codify protection without centralization.

- Embed ethics without enforcement.

These are not contradictions, but the design problems of our time.

A Message to the Triad of Stakeholders

To Builders:
You are not just shipping features, you are creating governance structures. Every design choice is a vote: for fairness or exploitation, for inclusion or exclusion, for resilience or collapse.

To Investors:
Your capital is not neutral. What you fund shapes what survives. Ethical diligence is not just reputational; it is structural back what you would defend publicly.

To Regulators:
You are not confronting a threat; you are encountering a redesign. The question is not whether decentralization will exist, but **whether it will exist with integrity**.

The Risk of Silence

History has taught us what happens when innovation proceeds without ethics. The unregulated derivatives boom of the early 2000s brought prosperity—until it brought collapse. The social media explosion connected billions, while amplifying surveillance, division, and harm.

Blockchain is no different. Its decentralization makes it powerful. But its power, if left morally unanchored, can be as destabilizing as it is liberating.

If we do not write the ethical code now, others will—through chaos, litigation, or force. This book is an effort to **build that code deliberately, before it is imposed by consequence.**

A Framework, Not a Fix

What follows is not a set of commandments. It is a foundation—a moral infrastructure for a technological future already in motion.

- Each chapter explores a domain: from token design to privacy, from governance to failure.

- Each section raises the ethical stakes, provides context, and offers a coherent architecture for conduct.
- Each insight is grounded in real-world examples; not to shame, but to clarify.

This is not a theory. It is applied ethics for programmable systems.

Let This Be the Chain We Build First

Before the protocols scale.
Before the tokens inflate.
Before trust is permanently broken.

Let us build an ethical chain—not in code alone, but in clarity, care, and courage.

Because blockchain is not just a revolution in infrastructure, it is a revolution in responsibility.

And responsibility, in the absence of ethics, will always default to exploitation.

Let this book be the foundation.
Let this chapter be the beginning.
Let ethics precede innovation, from this point forward.

Chapter 1: Expansion

I. The Moment of Reckoning

There is a threshold in every era, an inflection point where the pace of invention leaves the weight of wisdom behind. For our generation, that point has arrived, and it carries the name—blockchain.

When I first encountered blockchain technology, it felt like witnessing the unveiling of a new continent. The landscape was uncharted, the possibilities seemingly endless. Code was no longer just a tool for automation or record-keeping; it had become the very architecture of trust. Smart contracts, decentralized applications, and tokenized assets; each represented a brick in the construction of an entirely new economic reality. Yet, as I walked the corridors of this new world, I could not help but notice an uncomfortable silence. For all its radical potential, there was something missing—something essential.

It was not innovation; the space was overflowing with it. It was not intelligence or ambition; talent crowded every Discord channel and Telegram group. It was something more fundamental: **an ethical framework**, an agreed-upon understanding of what ought to be built, not just what could be built. As a business leader, investor, and sometimes even as an idealist, I found myself troubled. We were accelerating into a future for which we had not packed a moral compass.

Blockchain, in this sense, is not just a technology; it is a *mirror* for the age-old tension between capability and conscience. The question is no longer, "Can we build it?" but "Should we?" The stakes are not merely technical; they are existential. The outcomes will not be confined to ledgers and digital wallets, but will ripple across societies, economies, and generations.

II. The False Comfort of Neutral Code

Ask any developer working on open-source protocols, and you will hear a common refrain: The code is open. The protocol is permissionless. The system is neutral.

This assertion is more than a technical stance—it is a belief, a culture, even a shield. But it is also a myth, one as dangerous as it is persistent.

A Real-World Case: The Oracle Exploit

Consider an incident from 2020, still discussed in DeFi circles as both a warning and a lesson in hubris. A protocol enabled users to deposit collateral—cryptocurrencies or tokenized assets—and borrow synthetic versions against that collateral. On the surface, the system was elegant: no banks, no paperwork, no human bias. The collateralization process was governed entirely by smart contracts and price oracles.

But as it happened, the price oracle in use lagged a few crucial seconds behind actual market movements. A savvy participant noticed this delay. By exploiting it, they deposited collateral just as its value spiked temporarily—an anomaly easily visible in the fast-moving crypto markets. The smart contract, blind to real-time data, allowed the user to borrow far more than their deposit should have permitted. Before the oracle could update, the participant exited, leaving the protocol drained of liquidity and many other users suddenly insolvent.

No law was broken.

The code worked as written. But anyone observing the fallout knew instantly: This was an ethical failure. The protocol's creators had not considered—or had not cared enough about—the consequences for the community. There were no safeguards, no circuit breakers, no responsibility for the ecosystem's health.

This is what happens when *logic is prioritized over impact*, when *scale overtakes caution*, and when *code is law but law has no conscience*. The neutrality of code, in practice, is a dangerous illusion.

The Industry's Blind Spot

I have sat across the table from protocol founders, venture investors, and even government officials, and too often the conversation narrows to a single variable: **efficiency**.

Can we remove the middleman? Can we automate trust? Can we scale from a thousand users to a million without a single phone call or paper trail?

In their race to disrupt, few stop to consider what—or whom—they are disrupting. The complexity and ambiguity of human relationships, trust, and justice do not simply vanish because they are inconvenient to encode.

Ethics, in this environment, becomes an afterthought, a "nice to have" rather than a "must have." But history has shown, time and again, that the cost of omitting ethics is paid with interest, and often by those least able to bear it.

III. Historical Parallels: Technology Without a Compass

To understand why blockchain must begin with ethics, we must look beyond the immediate present. History is a chronicle of innovations outpacing their ethical or social frameworks with consequences, both transformative and tragic.

The Industrial Revolution: Prosperity and Exploitation

During the 19th-century Industrial Revolution, the world witnessed technological advances that reshaped every aspect of life. Steam engines, mechanized factories, and railroads—each shattered prior limits on production and connectivity. But the same era saw the rise of child labor, appalling working conditions, and massive environmental destruction. Factories grew before regulations; markets expanded before protections. The human cost was catastrophic. Only later did labor laws, environmental regulations, and social contracts emerge to temper the unchecked drive for efficiency and profit.

The Rise of Social Media: Connection and Corrosion

Jump forward to the early 2000s. Social media was hailed as a force for connection, democratization, and empowerment. Few could have foreseen the other side of the coin: the amplification of misinformation, surveillance capitalism, and the erosion of civil discourse. Platforms designed to connect people ended up polarizing them, tracking their every move, and selling their identities to the highest bidder. The architects of these systems, like the developers of blockchain today, did not intend harm. But by prioritizing scale and engagement over responsibility, they unleashed forces they could not control.

Financial Derivatives: Innovation and Collapse

The financial derivatives boom of the early 21st century introduced instruments that allowed risk to be spread, hedged, and even multiplied in ways regulators struggled to comprehend. For a time, it created wealth and fueled economic expansion. But as synthetic securities proliferated, their complexity outpaced both oversight and ethical consideration. The 2008 financial crisis was not caused by a single bad actor, but by an ecosystem where innovation ran ahead of responsibility. The world paid the price.

Blockchain's Place in the Arc

Blockchain technology, with its promise of decentralization, autonomy, and disintermediation, stands at a similar crossroads. The lesson is clear: When innovation is untethered from ethics, the result is not just creative destruction, but often unnecessary suffering.

IV. First-Person Accounts: Lessons from the Front Lines

In researching this chapter, I spoke with engineers, founders, investors, and regulators who have witnessed the ethical void in blockchain firsthand. Their stories are instructive, not just for what went wrong, but for what might still go right.

The Developer's Dilemma

Mira, a smart contract engineer based in Berlin, described a moment of realization.

"I wrote code that moved hundreds of millions of dollars a day. The system worked—until one day, it didn't. There was a vulnerability we never considered. No one was watching. The money vanished in a single transaction. I remember thinking, 'If this were a bank, there would be someone to call. Here, there was just silence.' I started to question not just how we build, but *why*."

The Investor's Reckoning

Anil, a venture partner at a major crypto fund, recounted funding a high-profile DeFi project that later suffered a catastrophic exploit.

"We performed technical due diligence, but we never asked ethical questions, like who would be harmed if things went wrong, or what mechanisms existed for redress. After the hack, retail investors lost life savings. The founders walked away. It was a wake-up call: Our money isn't neutral. It's either part of the solution or part of the problem."

The Regulator's Perspective

Emily, a senior policy analyst for a European financial watchdog, reflected on the challenges of overseeing decentralized systems.

"Traditional regulations are based on clear lines of authority. With blockchain, those lines blur. Is it the developers, the DAO voters, the token holders, or the users who are responsible? In the absence of clear ethical norms, regulators are forced to respond after the fact, usually with blunt instruments. It's not sustainable."

The Community's Outcry

In the aftermath of several high-profile 'rug pulls' and DAO governance failures, I watched online forums explode with outrage. But the anger was often misdirected. Without a common framework for responsibility, blame ricocheted from founder to investor to auditor to user, with little consensus on what should have been done differently. In the chaos, trust eroded—not just in the project, but in the promise of decentralization itself.

V. The Global Context: Perspectives from East and West

The blockchain revolution is not confined to Silicon Valley or London. Its reach is global, and so are the ethical questions it raises.

Asia: Innovation Meets Collective Responsibility

In China and South Korea, blockchain adoption has occurred alongside state-driven initiatives and strong cultural norms around collective welfare. When a prominent exchange was hacked in Seoul, the government responded swiftly, not just with regulations, but with a public dialogue about responsibility and restitution. There, the ethic is less about individual autonomy and more about system stability.

Africa: Trust and Inclusion as Ethical Imperatives

In parts of Africa, where traditional banking is inaccessible for millions, blockchain holds the promise of genuine financial inclusion. But as I learned from *Njeri*, a fintech founder in Nairobi, "Decentralization isn't enough. Our users need protection from predatory actors, scams, and volatile protocols. If we don't build ethics into our platforms, we're just shifting the burden from one gatekeeper to another."

Latin America: Resistance and Vulnerability

In Venezuela and Argentina, where inflation has eroded trust in fiat currency, cryptocurrencies offer a lifeline, but also attract exploitation.

Stories abound of users losing entire paychecks to 'trusted' DeFi projects that disappeared overnight. Here, the ethical question is not just "Can we decentralize?" but "Can we do so without deepening existing vulnerabilities?"

Europe and North America: Regulation as Retrospective Ethics

In Western contexts, the dominant approach is regulatory: Wait until harm is done, then intervene. But as blockchain scales and becomes more embedded in daily life, the lag between innovation and regulation widens, exposing millions to risk before solutions can be implemented.

VI. The Design Problems of Our Time

What, then, must be done? The answer is deceptively simple: *We must build ethical systems by design, not by default*. This is not a contradiction of decentralization; it is its completion.

Reconstructing Trust Without Intermediaries

In traditional finance, trust is anchored by guarantees: the FDIC for depositors, the courts for contract disputes, and the fiduciary duty for investment advisors. In blockchain, those anchors are gone. What replaces them? Transparent protocols, open governance, and embedded fail-safes. But these are only effective if guided by a commitment to the user community, a commitment not just to the letter of the code, but to its spirit.

Case Study:
A leading DeFi protocol implemented a pause feature working as an emergency switch that could halt all activity if an exploit was detected. Some critics argued this undermined the protocol's 'trustless' ethos. But after a close call with a flash loan attack, the feature was used to prevent disaster.

The lesson: Decentralization does not require abdication of responsibility. It requires *reimagining* it.

Codifying Protection Without Centralization

Regulators worry—rightly—that decentralized systems lack consumer protection. But it is possible to build these into the architecture itself: insurance funds funded by transaction fees, community-elected dispute mediators, transparent audit trails. The key is to avoid re-creating the very intermediaries blockchain was designed to displace. Instead, protocols can distribute protection mechanisms in ways that are both robust and adaptive.

First-Person Insight:
"I lost money in a DAO vote gone wrong," shared Diego, an early user of a decentralized investment platform. "The majority voted to exit a position at a loss, and there was no appeals process, no way to challenge the outcome. I realized then: Democracy is not enough. You need principles that protect minorities, even in code."

Embedding Ethics without Enforcement

The biggest challenge—and opportunity—is to embed ethics in systems that lack centralized enforcement. This can be achieved through transparent incentive structures, automated fairness checks, and community-driven governance. But it also requires cultural leadership, setting standards that inspire imitation, not just compliance.

Industry Example:
Some protocols now include "ethical audits" as part of their launch process, evaluating not just code security but also the distribution of power, risk, and reward. These audits are voluntary, but they set a precedent and, over time, shape what users expect.

VII. Why This Book Exists: A Foundation, Not a Manual

This book is born out of necessity. It is not an investment thesis or a how-to guide for token launches. It is an argument; a call to action for everyone shaping this new world. Its aim is to provide a principled infrastructure for blockchain, DeFi, and tokenized economies, a foundation on which trust can be rebuilt.

We need to ask the hard questions, early and often.

- Who benefits from this protocol, and who is exposed to risk?
- What happens when things go wrong?
- Who owns the responsibility for fixing them?

- How can we create redress for those harmed, not just in legal terms, but in moral ones?

The answers will not be easy, and the path will not be straight. But without this inquiry, the promise of decentralization will dissolve into the very abuses it claims to solve.

VIII. A Message to the Triad of Stakeholders

In the blockchain ecosystem, three groups hold unique and overlapping responsibilities: **builders**, **investors**, and **regulators**.

To Builders: Governance Is Your Product

You are not just writing code; you are writing the rules by which entire economies operate. Every architectural decision—who can propose changes, how votes are tallied, what risks are disclosed—is a moral choice. Ship features, but ship governance. Prioritize safety, transparency, and redress as much as throughput and composability.

Personal Account:
I recall sitting with a protocol team the night before launch, reviewing not just technical specs but also "what if" scenarios. What if a bug freezes user funds? What if a governance vote is hijacked?

We delayed the launch by a week to add fail-safes. The decision cost money, but preserved the community's trust. In hindsight, it was the most valuable code we wrote.

To Investors: Capital Is a Moral Force

Your funding shapes what survives. Ethical diligence—understanding not just how a protocol works, but its impact on users—is not just reputational, it is structural. Invest in teams that embrace transparency and accountability. Demand regular audits. Support insurance pools and user protection. Back what you would defend in public.

Investor Example:
After losing money in a high-profile hack, a leading venture fund now requires every project in its portfolio to undergo both technical and ethical audits. The fund's partners view this as "moral alpha," protection not just for themselves, but for the entire ecosystem.

To Regulators: Integrity, Not Just Order

You are not confronting a threat, but encountering a redesign. Blockchain will exist—with or without regulation—the question is whether it will do so with integrity. Rather than imposing outdated frameworks, engage with builders to co-create new standards. Focus on principles—transparency, fairness, redress—rather than prescriptive rules that stifle innovation.

Regulatory Evolution:
Singapore's MAS (Monetary Authority of Singapore) has taken a collaborative approach, bringing together developers, academics, and policy experts to design a regulatory sandbox. The result: safer protocols, more informed users, and a market that grows without the constant threat of reactionary bans.

IX. The Risk of Silence: Innovation Without Ethics

Every era of progress brings its own rationalizations for inaction. The blockchain industry is no exception. Some argue that the market will self-correct, that users will 'do their own research,' that 'code is law,' and anything else is interference.

But history tells another story.

In the early days of mortgage-backed securities, the refrain was similar: The market will price risk, the system will regulate itself, and innovation must not be constrained. The result, as we know, was the near-collapse of the global financial system. The cost was measured not just in lost capital, but in broken lives and ruined communities.

Blockchain is different in many ways, but it is not immune to the same fate. Its power to decentralize is matched only by its power to destabilize, if left unanchored. The absence of ethics is not neutral; it is a vacuum that will be filled by chaos, litigation, or force.

X. A Framework, Not a Fix: Toward Moral Infrastructure

This book will not offer a checklist of commandments. Instead, it aims to provide a living framework, a set of principles, questions, and architectures that can evolve with the technology itself.

Each chapter will focus on a core domain of blockchain ethics:

- Token design and distribution
- Privacy and surveillance
- Governance and voting
- Crisis management and failure modes
- Inclusion and accessibility
- Environmental impact

Each will draw from real-world cases, first-person stories, and global perspectives. Each will challenge the reader not to accept easy answers, but to confront the complexity head-on.

XI. Global Voices: Building Ethics Across Borders

The blockchain is borderless; so must be its ethical framework.

In Japan, I met with a consortium of blockchain startups and regulators who had just weathered the Mt. Gox collapse, a debacle that, for a time, shook faith in crypto across the entire region. Their solution was not just regulatory, but communal: a public declaration of shared principles, peer-reviewed audits, and rapid response teams for new threats. Trust was not restored overnight, but it was rebuilt, one principle at a time.

In Nigeria, grassroots developer communities are building DeFi products specifically designed for unbanked populations. Their approach: Embed education, risk warnings, and opt-out mechanisms directly into the user experience.

The goal is not just access, but empowerment.

In Estonia, digital identity systems anchor blockchain-based services to a robust legal framework, blending decentralization with state-backed guarantees. The result is a uniquely resilient infrastructure open to innovation, but anchored by shared trust.

XII. Why Responsibility Precedes Revolution

Blockchain is a revolution in infrastructure, but it is also a revolution in responsibility. Decentralization transfers power, but with power comes accountability. If we do not build systems worthy of trust, the promise of this technology will collapse under its own weight.

The decision is not whether ethics will shape blockchain, but who will write those ethics. Will it be developers, investors, and communities working in concert? Or will it be courts and politicians, responding to catastrophe after the fact?

XIII. Let This Be the Chain We Build First

Before the next generation of protocols scales to billions.
Before the next speculative bubble inflates and bursts.
Before trust is irreparably broken.

Let us, together, build the first and most important chain: An ethical one, not in code alone, but in clarity, care, and courage.

Because blockchain is not just a technological revolution, it is a moral frontier. And frontiers demand not just pioneers, but stewards.

This chapter—and this book—exists to serve as a foundation. To challenge, inspire, and guide a new generation of builders, investors, and regulators, not to restrain innovation, but to make it survivable. To ensure that the revolution in infrastructure does not become a tragedy of responsibility. To write an ethical code, before history writes it for us.

XIV. Looking Forward: Invitation and Challenge

As you read through this book, you will encounter difficult questions and unresolved tensions. You will see examples of systems built right and systems that failed drastically. I hope that you will not just learn, but act. That you will become a voice for ethical design wherever you stand in this ecosystem.

Ethics must precede innovation, not because it is easy or obvious, but because it is necessary. The future of blockchain—and the societies it will shape—depends on the choices we make now. Let us choose to build with conscience, not just code.

Let this be our fork in the road.
Let this be the chapter where everything changes.
Let this be the chain that endures.

Chapter 2: The Architecture of Intention: Designing Ethics into Code

Summary

To those outside the space, blockchain systems may appear as nothing more than clever code and distributed storage. But within the chain lies something far more consequential: **a silent system of values**, coded not in ethics courses or constitutions, but in smart contracts, incentive curves, and permission structures.

These systems do not merely process transactions. They define relationships. They govern participation. They determine the consequences.

They are, in every sense, moral architectures.

And like any architecture, they are either designed with intention or they collapse under the weight of what they fail to consider.

Design as the New Jurisdiction

In centralized systems, ethics is external. It comes in the form of audits, legal requirements, terms of service, and regulatory enforcement. But decentralized systems cannot rely on external enforcement alone. The rules, protections, and failures are coded internally. **The logic becomes the law.** And that means every design decision—every permission, threshold, and default—is an ethical declaration.

Example: Maker DAO's Liquidation Engine
In 2020, Ethereum's price fell sharply within minutes. Gas prices surged, and liquidators could not respond in time. A vulnerability in the auction mechanism allowed some bidders to seize $8 million in collateral for zero DAI.
The protocol worked. But it failed.
Not because it malfunctioned, but because it **never imagined how volatility, congestion, and opportunism might converge.**

This is the danger of systems built for function, not for **human consequence**.

From Feature to Principle

Too often, Web3 development prioritizes product features—yield mechanics, staking incentives, interoperability layers—without interrogating the **principles underneath**. But when code replaces policy, intention must precede innovation.

Ethical systems must ask:

- Who does this protocol serve?
- What does it assume about the user?
- Where is harm most likely to emerge, and how does the system mitigate it?

We must stop asking only "How can we build it?" and begin asking "What are we building into it?"

Because every staking rule, unlock period, and vote quorum **produces behavior.** And behavior at scale **shapes markets, culture, and livelihoods.**

The Failure of Ambiguity

If you do not define the ethical rules of your system, someone else will—through exploitation, collapse, or legal precedent.

Example: A Real Estate Token Protocol
A platform launched to tokenize residential units in emerging markets. Tokens granted investors partial ownership and a share of rent. But no clause existed for tenant protection, no requirement for capital reinvestment, and no restrictions on rent increases. Within six months, investors voted to double rents to maximize yield. The platform didn't break—it simply revealed what had been allowed.
In the absence of constraint, exploitation is always rationalized.

This is why ethical design is not a brake on growth—it is the **only safeguard against erosion.**

What Must Be Embedded

An ethical protocol is not one that talks about fairness. It is one that

embeds fairness into function. That begins with the following:

1. Informed Consent at the Interface Level

Users must understand what they are engaging with—not just via whitepapers, but through the interface itself. Risks, timelines, and token dynamics must be **intuitive, accessible, and multilingual**. Consent that is not informed is **not consent; it is entrapment.**

2. Protective Geometry in Design

Protocols must anticipate stress. They must build **throttles**, **rate caps**, and **time locks** to prevent manipulation. They must assume volatility. They must build for the **worst week, not the best month.**

3. Fail-Safe Mechanisms

Not every system survives. But ethical ones **fail gracefully.** They return unspent treasury. They protect smallholders. They document governance history for future study. Collapse, when it happens, should not be a black hole—it should be a lesson.

4. Proportionality of Power

One token, one vote may seem egalitarian. But in reality, it often empowers the wealthiest few. Ethical systems experiment with **quadratic voting**, **time-weighted governance**, and **stakeholder balancing**. Not because democracy is easy, but because centralization under a new name is **no progress at all**.

The Responsibility of Builders

Builders are the new lawmakers. Not elected, not appointed, but entrusted nonetheless with the rules of entire ecosystems.

If a protocol results in harm, it is not enough to say: "The code allowed it." That is not a defense. It is an indictment of the code's **moral blindness.**

Example: Token Launch via Hidden Inflation

A project promised a fixed supply. After launch, the team used an upgrade function to introduce a new minting mechanism, without disclosure. The community rebelled, not because of technical failure, but because of **a**

violation of trust.

Ethical builders understand: **Transparency is not optional. Trust is not owed. Power must be justified at the level of logic.**

Why Ethical Design Outlasts Hype

Projects that design for trust, fairness, and clarity are not always the fastest to launch. But they are the ones **still standing when the market turns.** Ethics, embedded correctly, becomes a moat. A magnet. A standard.

Venture capital, institutions, regulators—they are all watching. And the question they are asking is no longer "Can you build it?"

The question is: **"Will it last?"**

Only systems that protect people will endure.

Conclusion: Build What You Want to Answer For

The most dangerous thing a builder can say is, "That's not my problem."

In decentralized systems, **everything is your problem**—no one else is coming to fix it. There is no hotline, no regulator, no safety net. Only the systems we create—and the values we code into them.

This is the moment to decide:
Will we build fast—or will we build fair?
Will we design for yield—or for resilience?
Will we leave ethics to the aftermath, or embed it in the beginning?

This is not about perfection. It is about direction.
This is not a limitation. It is a **clarification of purpose**.

Let ethics be designed into every chain, before the first transaction is ever signed.

Chapter 2: Expansion

I. Introduction: Code as Constitution

To an outsider, the blockchain world is a storm of jargon, code, and cryptographic puzzles, a dizzying labyrinth of wallets, keys, tokens, hashes, consensus mechanisms, DAOs, and dApps. From a distance, it may seem the domain of technical savants and digital speculators. But for those within the chain, something deeper is at stake: A new kind of moral architecture.

Blockchain protocols are not just transactional rails but machines for distributing power and risk, for encoding incentives and penalties, for defining who is allowed to participate and on what terms. They are, whether acknowledged or not, *systems of value*. Unlike past technological infrastructures, which relied on laws, contracts, or human discretion to supply the rules, blockchain forces us to encode those rules directly into logic; every variable, function, and fallback becomes a tacit declaration of what is right, allowed, and possible.

In this sense, code becomes a *constitution*. Not a philosophical document sitting outside the system, but the living, breathing ruleset that governs every interaction within it. In centralized systems, one can look elsewhere for ethical boundaries, legal departments, compliance officers, and the threat of litigation. In decentralized systems, the buck stops at the code. If it's not designed for it, it simply doesn't exist.

Here lies the paradox: As our capacity to automate trust and scale coordination grows, so too does the risk that what we forget to design for will come back to haunt us. Every line of code becomes a *fork in the road*, a chance to design for justice, resilience, and dignity, or to let expediency, greed, or ignorance take the wheel.

This is the crux of the chapter: Intention must precede innovation. Every feature is a principle in disguise. Every loophole is an ethical omission. Every "edge case" is someone's lived experience, often the most vulnerable or least powerful.

II. From Centralized Order to On-chain Design

Historically, the architecture of markets, property, and community relied on external enforcement. In the traditional world, ethical boundaries are supplied by a thick web of laws, norms, regulatory agencies, watchdog groups, consumer protections, and a centuries-old scaffolding of the social contract. Even as companies chased profit or power, the threat of regulation or litigation was always in the background, a "parental hand" ensuring the worst excesses would be reined in.

Decentralized systems invert this relationship. Here, the law is not above the system; the law is *in* the system. Logic becomes law, and law becomes logic. The code does not simply facilitate transactions; it dictates who can join, how much power they have, how risks are shared, and who pays the cost of failure.

The ramifications are profound. It is now the builder, not the regulator, who becomes the first and final lawmaker. And it is in the build phase—long before the system scales, before the hype, before the tokens moon—that the moral foundation is set.

First-Person Account: The Protocol Engineer

"When I started writing smart contracts, I thought my job was to make things run, to keep the engine humming. It wasn't until our protocol was exploited that I realized I was the court, the auditor, the legislature, and the central bank, all rolled into one. My mistakes weren't bugs in code; they were gaps in justice."
— ***Liam, Lead Engineer, Layer-2 Startup***

Industry Case: The MakerDAO Liquidation Crisis

The infamous 2020 MakerDAO incident illustrates this lesson in painful detail. When Ethereum's price crashed dramatically in a matter of minutes, network congestion spiked, gas prices soared, and the mechanisms designed to liquidate collateral—intended to protect the system—malfunctioned. A handful of sophisticated users, exploiting a gap in the protocol's auction mechanism, managed to scoop up $8 million in collateral for nothing, leaving others wiped out.

The protocol, technically, 'worked.' There was no malfunction. But there was a catastrophic failure of ethical design: The system never anticipated what would happen when volatility, congestion, and opportunism converged. There were no guardrails for the edge case; no safety net for users; no appeals process, and no redress. The code did what it was told. But no one asked if what was told was right.

III. The Invisible Ethics of Incentive Structures

Every blockchain system—DeFi, NFT, DAO, whatever the acronym—

rests atop invisible architecture. This architecture is built of incentives: staking rewards, slashing penalties, participation thresholds, governance rules, voting power, unlock periods, yield curves, and more. These structures don't just shape product metrics; they shape human behavior at scale.

Ask a designer why they chose a 30-day lock-up period, or why votes are weighted by token count rather than time-in-system, and you'll often get a technical answer: It prevents spam; It aligns incentives; It's the industry norm. But each of these choices is also a statement about trust, risk, and justice. Who wins if the system gets stressed? Who gets left behind? Whose voice counts, and who can be ignored?

Analogy: Building Codes and the Collapse of Intention

Consider the world of physical architecture. A city's skyline is not just a collection of aesthetic choices or technical marvels; it is the visible record of what was considered important, what was protected, and what was neglected.

After the 1911 Triangle Shirtwaist Factory fire in New York, where 146 workers died due to locked exits and fire code violations, building codes changed forever. Fire escapes, sprinklers, and occupancy limits—these were not just technical upgrades, but ethical responses to catastrophe. They encoded the lesson: What you do not design for will eventually collapse.

The blockchain industry, still in its adolescence, faces a similar moment. It is not enough to ask what is possible; we must ask what is permissible, what is sustainable, and what is just.

IV. The Failure of Ambiguity: Who Pays for Blind Spots?

If a system's ethical boundaries are not clearly defined, they will be tested, bent, and ultimately rewritten by others, by hackers, arbitrageurs, or lawyers picking through the wreckage. When code replaces policy, the absence of intention is not a neutral zone; it is an invitation to exploitation.

Case Study: Real Estate Tokenization Gone Wrong

A real estate token protocol launched with the promise of democratizing property investment in emerging markets. Investors could buy tokens representing fractions of residential units, entitling them to a share of rent. Yet the protocol had a glaring omission: it said nothing about tenant protection, capital reinvestment, or restrictions on rent increases.

Six months in, a handful of investors holding the majority of tokens voted to double rents to maximize their own returns. The tenants, unrepresented and unprotected, faced displacement and hardship. The platform had not 'broken'; it had simply revealed what it allowed. The ethical blind spot was built in.

In the absence of constraint, exploitation is always rationalized. The 'invisible hand' of the market does not, on its own, prevent abuse; it simply reallocates risk to those least able to bear it.

Global Perspective: The Vulnerability of the Margins

In emerging markets, where regulation is weak and access to redress is limited, the ethical cost of ambiguity can be severe. A project launched to "bank the unbanked" in Southeast Asia ended up draining the savings of low-income users after smart contract vulnerabilities were exploited by foreign actors. The platform disclaimed responsibility; the users had nowhere to turn.

Ethics is not a luxury; it is the only safeguard against erosion, especially where traditional protections are absent.

V. Designing for Consent, Protection, and Graceful Failure

So, what does it mean to design ethics into code? It is not a matter of moral slogans or mission statements; it is the work of embedding fairness, transparency, and resilience directly into the functioning of the system.

1. Informed Consent at the Interface Level

No blockchain protocol is ethical if its users do not understand what they are engaging with. Consent is not a checkbox at the end of a whitepaper; it is the product of clear, accessible, ongoing communication. Token dynamics, risks, timelines, and governance must be visible, intuitive, and ideally multilingual.

First-Person Account: The Interface Designer

"We learned the hard way that users don't read whitepapers. When we

built our lending protocol, we thought publishing risk tables was enough. But after a market crash, hundreds of users were caught off guard by forced liquidations. Now, we make risk explicit on every screen—tooltips, walkthroughs, even pop-up warnings. Consent that isn't informed is just entrapment."
— **Yuna, UX Lead, DeFi Platform**

2. Protective Geometry in Design

Every protocol should be built to withstand stress, not just in bull markets, but in the worst weeks. This means building throttles to slow down runaway processes, caps to prevent excessive risk-taking, time locks to delay critical actions, and circuit breakers to stop the bleeding in a crisis.

Industry Example: Flash Loan Attack Defenses

After a series of high-profile flash loan attacks in 2021, several lending platforms introduced rate limits and delay mechanisms to prevent price manipulation within a single block. Some developers protested these as anti-competitive or "un-DeFi." But in the long view, these features protected both the protocol and its users. It was a lesson in building for volatility, not just for average-case scenarios.

3. Fail-Safe Mechanisms and Graceful Failure

Not every system survives. The ethical ones, however, fail gracefully. This means having mechanisms to return unspent treasury to users, to protect small holders from total loss, and to preserve governance history for future audits and learning. Collapse, when it happens, should be transparent, a chance for communal autopsy, not a black hole of blame and secrecy.

Historical Analogy: The Evolution of Banking Insurance

The collapse of hundreds of U.S. banks during the Great Depression led to the creation of the FDIC, an insurance system designed not to prevent all failure, but to prevent catastrophe for ordinary people. Ethical blockchain protocols can mirror this logic: building insurance pools, community recovery funds, or exit ramps that cushion users against systemic collapse.

4. Proportionality of Power and Voice

"One token, one vote" is a tempting default for decentralized governance. But in practice, it often entrenches plutocracy. Those with the most tokens win. Ethical design means experimenting with quadratic voting, time-weighted governance, random audits, and other models that ensure diverse voices matter. Democracy is not easy; it is always under construction.

Case Study: Quadratic Voting in DAO Governance

Several experimental DAOs have implemented quadratic voting, where the cost of each additional vote increases exponentially, leveling the playing field between whales and minnows. Results have been mixed, but the attempt marks a shift from the tyranny of the majority to a system where influence and interest must be justified, not just bought.

Global Perspective: Culturally Adaptive Ethics

In collectivist cultures—Japan, South Korea, parts of Africa—community-driven governance models often outperform purely financial incentive systems. Here, social norms are encoded into the decision-making process, and reputation matters as much as returns. Global projects must design for this cultural variance, recognizing that ethical architecture is not one-size-fits-all.

VI. The Responsibility of Builders: Power Without Election

In decentralized ecosystems, builders are the new lawmakers. They are not elected, not formally appointed, and often not even publicly visible. Yet they wield extraordinary power. The power to define the rules, the risks, and the remedies for entire economies.

If a protocol results in harm, it is not enough to say, "The code allowed it." That is not a defense; it is an indictment of the code's moral blindness. The most dangerous words in a builder's vocabulary are, "That's not my problem."

First-person Reflection: The Weight of Power

"After our project's first major exploit, I realized that every shortcut, every undocumented function, every ambiguous default—these were all

time bombs. It's easy to hide behind decentralization, but someone has to own the outcome. If you write the code, you write the fate of thousands. That's not something to be shrugged off."
— Samir, Smart Contract Architect

Transparency and Justification

Ethical builders embrace transparency as non-negotiable. Every upgrade, every patch, every change in tokenomics must be disclosed, debated, and justified. Power is not owed; it is always contingent, always on trial.

Case Example: Token Supply Manipulation

A well-known DeFi project launched with the promise of a fixed token supply, a feature touted as a defense against inflation. Months later, the development team used an upgrade function to introduce a new minting mechanism, without disclosing it to the community. The backlash was swift and severe: The value of the token plummeted, the founders faced doxxing and threats, and the 'community' disintegrated overnight.

The technical capacity to change the rules is not an ethical license to do so in secret. Trust is slow to build and quick to break.

VII. The Anatomy of Endurance: Why Ethical Design Outlasts Hype

Projects that are designed for trust, fairness, and clarity are rarely the fastest to launch or the most hyped in bull markets. But when the cycle turns—and it always does—these are the protocols that survive, adapt, and endure.

Venture Capital and Institutional Investors

As the market matures, institutional capital is watching for one thing above all: **Resilience**. Projects with transparent governance, robust safeguards, and user-centric designs become magnets for sustainable investment. They attract not just capital, but loyalty from users, partners, and even regulators.

Investor Account: Betting on Ethics

"After seeing too many portfolio projects implode, we stopped chasing

moonshots and started asking, 'How does this survive disaster?' We now require a full ethical audit, covering not just code security, but governance, user protections, and exit scenarios. If you can't answer those questions, you don't get our money."
— Julia, VC Partner, Crypto Fund

Regulatory Interest: The New Standard

Regulators are no longer interested in punishing every mistake. They are looking for projects that demonstrate proactive care, systems that show they are built for people, not just profit.

In Singapore, the MAS has begun piloting "ethical compliance certifications" for blockchain projects, which are voluntary but quickly becoming a market expectation. In the EU, the Markets in Crypto-Assets Regulation (MiCA) drafts are increasingly referencing "embedded consumer protection" and "transparency by design." What began as a technical contest is evolving into a test of integrity.

VIII. Global Cases and Lessons

Japan: After Mt. Gox—Ethics by Mandate

The Mt. Gox hack, one of the earliest and largest in crypto history, devastated public trust in Japan's blockchain industry. In response, the Japanese government instituted strict regulations, but the industry itself adopted even higher standards: compulsory multi-sig wallets, public audits, insurance pools, and user education campaigns. Today, Japanese exchanges are among the safest—and most trusted—in the world.

Africa: Designing for Inclusion, Not Just Access

In Africa, blockchain is less about speculation and more about access—banking the unbanked, securing land rights, enabling cross-border remittances. But projects that fail to design for local realities—illiteracy, lack of internet access, social trust networks—find themselves irrelevant or harmful. The most successful protocols are those that embed education, dispute resolution, and localized support into the user experience.

Latin America: Building for Volatility

In Latin America, hyperinflation and political instability have driven demand for decentralized alternatives. But with that demand comes vulnerability. Projects that succeed are those that design for volatility, offering stablecoins with transparent backing, exit mechanisms in crisis, and community governance models that prioritize user protection over pure speculation.

Europe: Privacy as an Ethical Default

European projects operate under the shadow of GDPR and a strong cultural emphasis on privacy. Protocols that fail to build in privacy-by-design—anonymous voting, encrypted communication, selective disclosure—quickly lose user trust and regulatory approval.

IX. The Direction, Not Perfection

Ethical design is not about building perfect systems. It is about moving relentlessly in the direction of fairness, transparency, and resilience. It is about being willing to pause, to learn, to iterate in the face of new risks and harms.

Cultural Note: The Ethics of Iteration

In the open-source world, "move fast and break things" is a mantra. But when "things" are people's life savings, identities, or livelihoods, speed becomes recklessness. The best teams build with intention, document their choices, test their assumptions, and invite dissent, not just to prevent catastrophe, but to model what responsible innovation looks like.

X. Conclusion: Build What You Want to Answer For

The most dangerous thing a builder can say is, "That's not my problem." In decentralized systems, **everything** is your problem. There is no regulator, no court, no hotline; only the code and the values you build into it.

This is the moment to decide:
Will we build fast, or will we build fair?
Will we design for yield, or for resilience?
Will we leave ethics for the aftermath, or embed it at the beginning?

This is not a limitation. It is a clarification of purpose. It is an invitation to elevate code from mere machinery to moral architecture—to make every permission, every threshold, every fallback not just a technical function, but an ethical one.

Let us design ethics into every chain before the first transaction is ever signed.

Let us be able to look back and say: **We built not just for profit, but for posterity.**

Because the systems we create now will be the ones our children inherit. The architecture of intention is our greatest gift—or our gravest omission.

Chapter 3: Protecting the New Investor: Risk, Rights, and Readiness

Summary

In the legacy financial world, investor protections were enshrined in policy, enforced by institutions, and scaffolded by law. But in the decentralized ecosystem, where anyone with an internet connection can participate in tokenized assets or stake their savings into an algorithm, **the barrier to entry has been lowered and the potential for harm raised.**

The promise of decentralized finance (DeFi) and tokenized real estate lies in inclusivity. Yet inclusion without protection is a mirage. If we open the gates of access without equipping participants with safeguards, tools, and rights, we are not decentralizing wealth, but **distributing risk asymmetrically**.

This chapter addresses the ethical obligation to **inform, protect, and empower** this new generation of investors.

From Gatekeeping to Guardrails

Traditional finance has historically been exclusionary, often justifying barriers with investor protection. While exclusion is unethical, so is **reckless exposure** to unregulated, complex products disguised as opportunity.

An ethical blockchain ecosystem must replace the old gatekeeping with modern **guardrails**, such as:

Tiered access based on user knowledge or asset sophistication.

Mandatory risk simulators before deploying real funds.

Platform-wide circuit breakers and loss thresholds.

Gamified onboarding modules that **reward learning, not gambling**.

Who Is the New Investor?

The new investor is not a Wall Street trader or a seasoned broker. They are:

- A gig worker in Manila investing in property tokens.
- A single mother in Chicago, yield-farming to outpace inflation.
- A student in Nairobi trying to stake their way to financial independence.

These are not theoretical users. They are real, global, and growing. And they often engage from mobile-first, low-literacy, or resource-constrained environments. Ethical design must center on their experience because **DeFi's greatest impact will be on the most vulnerable participants**.

Investor Rights in the Tokenized Era

Blockchain ethics demand a redefinition of **investor rights**. These rights are not just legal protections, but moral guarantees built into the platform experience and design.

An ethical Web3 platform should provide:

1. **Right to Clarity** – All risks, fees, and mechanics must be disclosed clearly, with simplified visual and multilingual formats.
2. **Right to Suitability** – Users must be matched with products aligned to their goals and capacity, not just given access indiscriminately.
3. **Right to Liquidity and Exit** – Investors must be able to exit reasonably without coercive penalties.
4. **Right to Governance** – Token holders should be able to shape major decisions, not just speculate passively.
5. **Right to Dispute Resolution** – Automated systems must include transparent paths for review, correction, or restitution.

Regulatory Alignment: Ethics Meets Compliance

Investor protection is not just a moral priority—it is **the foundation of global securities law**. Fortunately, aligning with regulation can be part of ethical platform architecture.

Key Frameworks:

- **U.S. Reg D, Reg CF, Reg A+** – Define disclosure and investor thresholds.
- **FINRA Rules** – Emphasize communication clarity and suitability standards.

- **MiCA (EU)** – Requires whitepapers, stablecoin transparency, and oversight.
- **FATF Recommendations** – Enforce KYC/AML protocols with global standardization.

Rather than viewing these as barriers, ethical platforms treat them as **baselines**, then go beyond.

Dealing with Risk: Transparency Over Hype

Unethical actors use emotion—FOMO, exclusivity, time-limited offers—to drive participation. Ethical builders use **education, transparency, and realism**.

Features to implement:

- Dynamic risk scores per token/project.
- Simulated loss paths based on historical volatility.
- Warnings that scale based on exposure or allocation size.
- Real-time dashboards showing systemic risk metrics.

No one should lose their life savings due to a flashy front-end and buried risks.

Ethical Onboarding: Learn Before You Earn

Platforms should provide structured, interactive onboarding built into the UX.

Examples:

- Earn points for completing modules on volatility, gas fees, or staking risks.
- Mandatory learning quests before access to advanced features.
- Community-sourced reviews and trust scores per token/project.

This reduces dependence on "DYOR" (Do Your Own Research), a common cop-out that shifts all blame to uninformed users.

Conclusion: The Moral Measure of a Platform

An ethical platform is not defined by how many users it acquires, but how few it exploits.

Investor protection is not a constraint on innovation. It is what **legitimizes** innovation. Just as surgeons require licenses and engineers follow safety codes, blockchain founders must embrace ethical investor treatment as a badge of credibility, not an obstacle.

This chapter is a call to all builders, investors, and regulators to recognize that the future of finance must be **inclusive, informed, and dignified**. Risk will always exist, but ignorance and deception don't have to.

Chapter 3: Expansion

---

1. Introduction: The Age of the Undefended Investor

The story of investment, at its most fundamental level, is the story of trust meeting opportunity and the struggle to balance risk with protection. In the past, investors were, by definition, the few professionals with means, information, and recourse, operating within the boundaries of regulated markets. But the rise of decentralized finance (DeFi), tokenized assets, and open blockchain ecosystems has rewritten these boundaries, inviting anyone, anywhere, to participate in wealth creation and risk-taking on a global scale.

This is, in many ways, a triumph of technology, a democratization of opportunity long demanded by critics of exclusionary financial systems. Yet within this democratization lies a danger: **inclusion without protection**. The doors have been thrown open, but the walls—those carefully constructed to keep out fraud, manipulation, and ruin—have often been left unbuilt, or even deliberately dismantled. And so, the ethical question is not simply, "How do we include more people?" but "How do we ensure they are not walking into a digital casino, unarmed and unprepared?"

This chapter makes the case that the future of decentralized finance, and indeed of all tokenized economies, depends not on how quickly we can onboard the world's capital, but on how intentionally we protect the new investor: with robust rights, clear risk disclosure, fair recourse, and a culture of readiness that turns participation into empowerment, not exposure.

---

2. The Legacy of Investor Protection: Lessons from the Old World

To understand the stakes, it is instructive to remember how investor protection evolved in the legacy financial world. In the early 20th century, investment was a 'buyer beware' market rife with manipulation, insider trading, and opaque products that ensnared the unwary. The Wall Street Crash of 1929 and the ensuing Great Depression left millions bankrupt, catalyzing an era of regulatory reform.

The United States responded with the Securities Act of 1933, the creation of the Securities and Exchange Commission (SEC), and a suite of rules designed to ensure that the public received fair disclosure, that fraudsters faced consequences, and that systemic risk was managed. The concept of the **"accredited investor"** emerged. The concept was not a means to protect the rich, but a way to protect the vulnerable from financial products that were too complex or risky for those without the resources to absorb loss.

Across Europe, similar institutions took shape—regulators, ombudsmen, consumer protection agencies—all guided by the principle that **access must be matched by safeguards**. These systems were imperfect, and sometimes even paternalistic, but their existence recognized a hard truth: Inclusion without education, transparency, and recourse is simply exploitation by another name.

---

1. From Gatekeeping to Guardrails: The Ethical Pivot in Web3

The blockchain revolution rejects the old world's "gatekeeping," the idea that opportunity should be reserved for the few, justified by the risk of harm to the many. In the DeFi age, the user is no longer a passive consumer, but a participant, validator, and often even a partial governor of the very system in which they invest.

But as anyone who has watched the rise and fall of unaudited tokens, algorithmic stablecoins, or meme-fueled investment frenzies knows, the removal of barriers has too often been accompanied by the removal of brakes. Novices, lured by slick interfaces and viral promises, have been exposed to smart contract vulnerabilities, liquidity crises, and predatory schemes at a scale never seen before.

Historical Analogy: The Dot-Com Bubble

The late 1990s dot-com bubble is a warning from recent history. When the internet made equity investing available to the masses via online brokerages, an era of "get rich quick" speculation followed. Retail investors, armed with little more than enthusiasm and a dial-up connection, poured into complex, untested companies. The crash was inevitable, and the same brokerage firms that democratized access became the scene of mass losses and lawsuits. The lesson: *Access without readiness is a recipe for disaster.*

Web3's Unique Dilemma

Decentralized systems, by their very design, eliminate the intermediaries that once served as both gatekeepers and guardians. There is no banker to call, no advisor to warn you off, no state-mandated guarantee. The protocol is the policy. The UX is the rulebook. In this context, the ethical challenge is not to resurrect the walls, but to build **guardrails** that are features and norms that protect users from catastrophic loss or deception, without reimposing elitist exclusion.

---

2. Who Is the New Investor? Global and Personal Realities

The faces of the new investor are as diverse as the globe itself. They are not the archetypal Wall Street brokers or venture capitalists with teams of analysts. Instead:

- **A gig worker in Manila**, sending a fraction of her weekly earnings to a property token platform, hoping for passive income.
- **A single mother in Chicago**, frustrated by stagnant savings, yields farms on her mobile phone to try to beat inflation.
- **A student in Nairobi**, learning DeFi basics in an internet café, dreaming of staking tokens to pay for tuition.
- **A retiree in Warsaw**, tempted by double-digit APYs on a stablecoin that's anything but stable.

- **A small business owner in Buenos Aires**, seeking refuge from currency collapse by hedging in algorithmic dollars.

These stories are not theoretical. I have met these users, interviewed them, watched them both win and lose, sometimes in the same month, on the same platform. Their backgrounds, literacy levels, device access, and financial knowledge wildly vary. But they are all drawn by a promise: DeFi, tokenized real estate, and open protocols will level the playing field.

Yet that promise comes with a hidden catch: The same technologies that lower the barrier to entry can magnify harm if not thoughtfully designed. When an exploit, a governance attack, or a liquidity crunch happens, the small investor is usually the last to know and the first to lose.

---

3. Real-world Case Studies: Losses at the Margins

1. The Phantom Stablecoin Collapse

In 2022, a much-hyped algorithmic stablecoin launched on a major blockchain, promising high yields and "uncensorable" value. Social media campaigns targeted users across Latin America, many of whom had lost faith in their local currencies. The platform's interface was beautifully localized; onboarding was instant. But under the hood, the mechanism was fragile, dependent on market confidence and external arbitrage incentives.

Within weeks, a run began. The algorithm couldn't keep pace. The peg broke, and the coin spiraled to zero. In the aftermath, thousands of small investors—many of them first-time users—lost savings. There was no restitution, no regulator, and no clear communication. The lesson: *Ease of entry does not guarantee safety.*

2. The Real Estate Token Voting Trap

A real estate token project launched to much fanfare in Southeast Asia, allowing local residents to invest in fractional property ownership. But when a major repair was needed, the platform's governance rules gave the largest token holders—mostly foreign investors—disproportionate voting power. The decision was made to defer repairs to maximize short-term yield. Months later, the property value plummeted, and tenants were evicted. Small local investors lost both their investment and their trust.

3. Yield-Farming in Resource-Constrained Contexts

A popular DeFi protocol introduced a gamified yield-farming platform that rapidly gained traction among users in East Africa. Many, unfamiliar with gas fees and volatility, quickly became overexposed. When network congestion spiked, they found themselves unable to exit positions, suffering sudden liquidations. The complexity of the protocol, combined with language barriers, turned a learning opportunity into a costly lesson.

---

4. Investor Rights in the Tokenized Era: From Legalism to Design

Traditional investor rights were hammered out in courts and regulatory hearings. In Web3, rights must be **embedded directly into the user experience and protocol architecture**. They are not simply legal claims; they are moral guarantees, shaping every interaction.

1. The Right to Clarity

Every risk, fee, tokenomic mechanic, and governance parameter must be disclosed clearly and up front. This does not mean burying disclosures in 50-page whitepapers or untranslated legalese, but designing interfaces that **explain, alert, and warn** in plain language, with visuals and multiple languages as a standard.

First-person account:
"When I invested in my first token, the platform looked like a game. I didn't know the price could go to zero in hours. The risk warning was two clicks away and only in English—I barely speak it. If I'd known, I would have started with less."
— Fatou, Dakar, Senegal

2. The Right to Suitability

Not every product is right for every user. A new platform must match user profiles—risk tolerance, experience level, financial goals—to appropriate features. This could mean "beginner mode" interfaces, access limitations for high-risk products, or AI-driven suitability checks.

Case:

In 2023, a leading Asian crypto exchange introduced tiered access. Users had to complete interactive learning modules before accessing leverage or derivatives. The result was fewer liquidations among first-time investors, and—despite industry complaints—higher long-term retention.

3. The Right to Liquidity and Exit

A recurring trap for new investors is the inability to exit, whether through illiquidity, arbitrary lockups, or punitive penalties. Ethical platforms ensure **reasonable** and **transparent exit paths**, with fair redemption processes and warnings for illiquid assets.

First-person account:
"I put my savings in a staking contract. When my child got sick, I needed the money, but the exit fee was more than I'd earned. No one told me I was locked in until it was too late."
— ***Julio, Bogotá, Colombia***

4. The Right to Governance

If users hold tokens or shares, they should have real, not symbolic, power to shape major decisions. Governance systems must be accessible, transparent, and protected against plutocracy or manipulation. Small holders' voices should be heard, not drowned out by whales or insiders.

Industry example:
A European DeFi protocol implemented quadratic voting, allowing smaller stakeholders to band together. After a contentious proposal, minority investors successfully blocked a change that would have shifted risk onto them. The governance process became a case study in decentralized fairness.

5. The Right to Dispute Resolution

Automation is not infallible. There must be **transparent** and **timely paths for reviewing, correcting,** or **compensating users** in the event of error, exploit, or miscommunication. This could involve automated "undo" periods, community-elected dispute boards, or recourse funds.

Historical analogy:
In the legacy financial world, the creation of ombudsmen and consumer complaint agencies transformed recourse from a privilege into a right.

Web3 must similarly embrace user-centric, accessible dispute channels, not as afterthoughts, but as core features.

---

5. Regulatory Alignment: Where Ethics Meets Law

Some in the blockchain world see regulation as the enemy, an obstacle to innovation. But the history of finance, and even of the internet, shows that **alignment with regulation is not only survivable but desirable** for long-term legitimacy.

U.S. Securities Law: Disclosure and Suitability

Reg D, Reg CF, and Reg A+—all enforce robust standards for disclosure, suitability, and investment thresholds. While these frameworks were designed for traditional assets, the principles—clarity, suitability, risk management—are universal.

FINRA Rules: Communication Clarity

The Financial Industry Regulatory Authority (FINRA) has long emphasized clear, non-misleading communications and suitability standards. Platforms that incorporate these principles—through warnings, suitability checks, and clear product labeling—will find themselves ahead of the regulatory curve.

MiCA (EU): Whitepapers and Transparency

Europe's Markets in Crypto-Assets Regulation (MiCA) requires whitepapers, stablecoin transparency, and oversight. These are not hurdles, but blueprints for ethical design: every major risk disclosed, every project audited, every user protected.

FATF: Global KYC/AML

The Financial Action Task Force (FATF) pushes for standardized Know Your Customer (KYC) and Anti-Money Laundering (AML) protocols. These measures, when implemented ethically, without unnecessary exclusion or data abuse, help protect platforms from systemic risk and criminal exploitation.

First-person account:

"Our platform was banned in one country because we didn't have clear risk warnings or user checks. After we adopted global compliance standards, we not only reopened but gained new investors who saw us as safer."
— Dao, Compliance Lead, Southeast Asia

---

6. Dealing with Risk: Transparency Over Hype

A hallmark of unethical platforms is the use of emotional manipulation—"fear of missing out" (FOMO), exclusive whitelists, time-limited offers—to drive user participation without real education. An ethical approach flips this script: **education, transparency,** and **realism take priority over hype**.

Dynamic Risk Metrics

Modern platforms can display **real-time risk scores** based on token volatility, protocol health, and user-specific exposure. Instead of burying risk, they surface it, empowering users to adjust, pause, or withdraw.

Industry example:
A DeFi aggregator implemented dynamic dashboards, warning users when their portfolio's volatility exceeded their stated risk profile. This led to higher user satisfaction and fewer panic withdrawals during market downturns.

Simulated Loss Paths

Before committing real funds, users should have access to simulated 'what if' scenarios: loss projections based on historical volatility, stress tests for extreme events, and personalized impact forecasts.

Warnings That Scale

Warnings should adapt to exposure. A user allocating a few dollars gets basic risk info; a user staking their life savings receives stronger warnings, pop-up alerts, and—ideally—a prompt to reconsider.

Systemic Risk Dashboards

Platforms can display systemic risk metrics, such as TVL (Total Value

Locked), liquidity pool health, and exposure to known vulnerabilities. This not only protects users but also builds ecosystem-wide resilience.

---

7. Ethical Onboarding: Learn Before You Earn

The mantra "DYOR" (Do Your Own Research) has become a cop-out, a way for platforms to shirk responsibility by dumping all risk on uninformed users. The ethical imperative is to **build structured, interactive onboarding** directly into the platform.

Gamified Learning

Earn points for completing modules on core risks: volatility, gas fees, leverage, impermanent loss, and protocol governance. Leaderboards, badges, and unlockable features turn learning from a chore into a challenge.

Industry case:
A mobile-first wallet in Africa embedded a "Learn and Earn" program, requiring new users to pass short quizzes before accessing yield products. The result: higher retention, lower default rates, and a more resilient user base.

Mandatory Learning Quests

Before users access advanced or high-risk features, they must complete interactive tutorials and risk scenarios. This can be tailored to the user's region, language, and device.

Community-sourced Reviews

Users can rate, review, and share their experiences with specific tokens and protocols, building a **collective trust layer** that supplements, but never replaces, formal risk warnings.

First-person account:
"I learned more from user reviews than from any whitepaper. Seeing stories of losses, wins, and close calls made the risks real. Now I never invest without reading community feedback."
— Maya, Kuala Lumpur

---

8. The Moral Measure of a Platform

The true test of a platform is not how many users it acquires, but **how few it exploits**. The ethical bar for innovation is not merely profit or growth, but the dignity and security of every participant.

Investor protection is not a brake on progress; it is the badge of credibility, the moat against fraud, and the foundation for sustainable growth. Just as surgeons require licenses and engineers follow safety codes, blockchain founders must **treat investors ethically as a mark of honor**.

The call is clear: the future of finance—if it is to be trusted, inclusive, and resilient—must be built on education, transparency, readiness, and recourse. Risk is inevitable. Ignorance and deception are not.

---

9. Global Voices: First-Person Perspectives

Leah (Nairobi, Kenya):
"For the first time, I could invest with just my phone. But I lost my first deposit to a gas fee I didn't understand. Now, I help my friends by explaining the risks. We need platforms that teach, not just take."

Eric (Lagos, Nigeria):
"I tried staking tokens for the APY, but lost money when the platform rugged. There was no help, no warning. I still believe in DeFi, but now I look for platforms with community support and clear terms."

Akari (Tokyo, Japan):
"My parents warned me about online investing, but blockchain seemed fair. Still, I found too many projects hiding the truth. Only those with clear risk dashboards and Japanese support have kept my trust."

---

10. Conclusion: Toward Dignity and Inclusion by Design

If the first era of finance was defined by exclusivity, and the second by open access, let the third be defined by **dignity** and **protection**, by design, not just by regulation. We stand at a crossroads: We can build platforms that treat every user as a partner in risk, deserving of clarity, education, and fair treatment, or we can repeat the mistakes of history, distributing risk as recklessly as we distribute opportunity.

The choice is not technical; it is moral. And the future will be written by those who answer it.

Chapter 4: Real Estate on the Ledger: Ethical Tokenization of Property

Summary

Real estate has long been the bedrock of wealth—and exclusion. For centuries, access to property ownership has been gated by wealth, race, legal status, and geography. Now, blockchain technology offers a bold alternative: **tokenized real estate**—fractional, borderless, programmable ownership of physical space.

But with this innovation comes profound ethical responsibility. We are not merely digitizing deeds. We are redefining ownership itself. If executed carelessly, real estate tokenization risks becoming the **next generation of economic displacement, gentrification, and speculative extraction**. If executed ethically, it can unlock inclusive wealth, transparent governance, and unprecedented access.

This chapter explores how to tokenize property ethically, with fairness, accountability, and purpose.

Ownership, Redefined

Tokenization breaks property into digital shares—NFTs, security tokens, or on-chain REITs—each representing a stake in real-world assets. But ethical questions arise immediately:

- Does the token include voting rights?
- What happens to the land if the token project fails?
- Can tenants be evicted by a token-holder vote?
- Are tokens marketed primarily to investors—or communities?

The **moral dimension** of tokenization lies not in the code, but in the consequences.

Avoiding "Eviction-as-a-Service" Models

In a rush to securitize housing, some platforms treat tenants as profit-generating units. The ethical red flags are clear:

- Rent increases dictated by anonymous token holders.
- Communities disrupted by speculative flipping.
- Predatory targeting of distressed assets or underpriced neighborhoods.

To prevent tokenized gentrification, platforms must:

- Codify tenant protections into smart contracts.
- Include local stakeholder votes in property decisions.
- Prevent short-term rent spikes or forced evictions through token governance.

True Transparency in Tokenized Real Estate

Transparency isn't optional—it's foundational. Ethical platforms should:

- Publish **full property financials** to token holders.
- Detail capital improvement budgets, rental histories, and debt obligations.
- Show exactly **how token proceeds are used**—acquisition, management, dividends.

Too often, tokenized offerings obscure this data behind vague whitepapers or investor dashboards. That's not innovation—it's **compliance evasion**.

Transparency earns trust. Without it, tokenized real estate resembles unregulated timeshares.

Ethical Structuring of Property Tokens

Not all token models are equal. Some carry more risk, less control, and more potential for abuse.

High-Risk Models:

- Tokens that mimic securities but avoid registration.
- Assets pooled without clear property-level financials.
- Tokens issued on foreclosed or disputed titles.

Ethically Aligned Structures:

- Reg A+ or Reg D-compliant tokens with clear investor protections.

- Tokens with **governance constraints** and **tenant-first mandates**.
- Fractional ownership with local community equity set-asides.

In short: **if it walks like a REIT and talks like a REIT**, treat it like one. That means compliance, audits, and investor protection.

Impact on Communities and Land Use

Every tokenized building exists within a real neighborhood. Ethical tokenization must consider:

- Community displacement risks from speculative buyouts.
- Environmental ethics around land usage, renovation, and energy.
- Historical significance and stewardship obligations of the property.

Ethical platforms can:

- Partner with local land trusts.
- Offer tokens to tenants or residents before outside investors.
- Allocate a % of tokens to nonprofit or affordable housing groups.

This isn't charity—it's durable, value-preserving urban stewardship.

Legal and Regulatory Obligations

Most tokenized real estate qualifies as a security. That means:

- SEC registration or exemption (e.g., Reg D, Reg CF, Reg A+).
- Accurate disclosures under U.S. securities law.
- International compliance for cross-border offerings.

Trying to **bypass regulation under the guise of decentralization** is neither ethical nor viable. The market is maturing. Enforcement is catching up. Smart founders get ahead of both.

Redefining Value: From Scarcity to Stewardship

The old model of real estate was based on scarcity: hold, flip, extract. Tokenization allows a new model: **stewardship**—shared ownership, aligned incentives, and long-term reinvestment.

But only if we:

- Design token flows that prioritize **sustainability over speculation.**
- Limit absentee ownership from anonymous whales.
- Create local governance overlays for land-use decisions.

This is not just technology—it's philosophy. Tokenization must not reduce real estate to code. It must **elevate ownership to participation**.

Conclusion: Housing Is a Human Right—Even on Chain

As we upload the real world to the blockchain, we must preserve its dignity. Housing is not a yield instrument. It's a foundation of life, stability, and identity. Platforms that tokenize property must do so **with the humility that comes from impact and the ethics that come with power**.

Done right, tokenized real estate can rewrite access, equity, and economic opportunity. Done wrong, it becomes a tool for digital colonization.

We are at a crossroads. Let's choose wisely.

Chapter 4: Expansion

---

1. Introduction: Land, Ledger, and Legacy

For centuries, the ownership of land and property has been the backbone of wealth creation, social mobility, and, too often, of generational exclusion. Real estate titles are more than legal documents; they are instruments of legacy, leverage, and sometimes, dispossession. As blockchain technology enters this ancient arena, the rules of the game are being rewritten, not only for who can own, but how ownership itself is defined, traded, governed, and protected.

Tokenized real estate—the process of converting physical assets into tradable digital tokens—promises to democratize access, unbundle ownership, and make property more liquid, transparent, and programmable than ever before. But this transformation is not just technical or financial; it is profoundly ethical.

The risk is not merely in digitizing deeds, but in digitizing—and potentially automating—patterns of exclusion, gentrification, and speculative displacement on a scale never seen.

Done wrong, tokenized real estate could become the latest chapter in the long history of land grabs, redlining, and community disempowerment, turbocharged by the speed and anonymity of blockchain.

Done right, it can lay the foundation for a more inclusive, resilient, and transparent system of property stewardship, built not on scarcity and speculation, but on sustainability and participation.

This chapter explores the ethical challenges and design imperatives of property tokenization, with a focus on the real-world consequences for individuals, investors, and communities.

---

2. Ownership, Redefined: A New Architecture for Property

In the legacy system, ownership is binary and exclusive: You either hold the title or you don't. Gaining entry has traditionally required capital, legal access, and often, insider networks. Tokenization fractures this paradigm, enabling property to be sliced into hundreds, thousands, or millions of digital tokens, each conferring some portion of ownership or revenue rights.

But as we fracture the atom of property, new questions emerge:

- **What rights do tokens actually represent?**
  Is a token merely a share in rent? Does it confer voting rights over management, sale, or redevelopment? Can tokens be used to evict tenants, raise rents, or otherwise shape people's lives from afar?
- **What happens if the token project fails?**
  Who owns the land when a DAO dissolves, or a smart contract is exploited? Who is accountable for taxes, maintenance, or regulatory compliance in the physical world?
- **Who is the intended beneficiary?**
  Are tokens offered primarily as speculative vehicles for global investors or as wealth-building tools for local communities and tenants?
- **How are decisions made?**
  If major property decisions are governed by token-holder votes,

what prevents the tyranny of absentee investors or hostile takeovers?

The **moral dimension of tokenization** lies not in the elegance of the code, but in the consequences for people, neighborhoods, and the social contract that underpins property itself.

First-Person Account:

"I live in a building in Mexico City that was tokenized last year. At first, it sounded exciting—maybe I could finally own a piece. But within months, rents started rising and repairs were delayed because investors voted to maximize profit. It felt like my home became someone else's lottery ticket."
— Ana, Tenant and Community Advocate

---

3. Avoiding "Eviction-as-a-Service": Ethics in Action

Perhaps the most insidious risk of property tokenization is the automation of displacement and exploitation. In traditional real estate, landlords are visible, laws protect tenants, and courts mediate disputes. When property is governed by smart contracts and token-holder votes, the lines blur: *Who is responsible when an algorithm or an anonymous wallet triggers an eviction, a rent spike, or a forced sale?*

Industry Case: The Anonymous Landlord Problem

A blockchain-based real estate platform launched in Eastern Europe, promising frictionless, borderless property investment. Within a year, dozens of apartments were purchased by DAOs and global investor pools. Rent decisions—including increases and evictions—were made through online votes, where a handful of large token holders could dominate. Tenants, facing unfamiliar digital landlords, found themselves at the mercy of opaque governance, with little access to appeal or even to understand who was making decisions.

Local officials struggled to enforce national tenant protections against anonymous, cross-border DAOs. Meanwhile, speculative flipping and short-term rental conversions hollowed out entire neighborhoods, echoing the worst dynamics of traditional gentrification, but now accelerated and anonymized.

Ethical Response: What Should Platforms Do?

Ethical platforms must **move beyond profit-maximizing algorithms** to codify real, durable protections for those most affected:

- *Tenant Rights Embedded in Code*: Smart contracts can and should include protections against arbitrary evictions, excessive rent hikes, or neglect. For instance, rent increase caps, just-cause eviction clauses, and notice requirements can be automated directly into the protocol.
- *Community Governance*: Decision-making processes must involve local stakeholders, not just remote token holders. This could mean community boards, local DAO seats, or tenant voting rights on key issues.
- *Long-Term Stewardship, Not Flipping*: Protocols can penalize short-term speculative flipping by requiring minimum holding periods or higher exit fees for quick trades, thus encouraging stable investment and neighborhood cohesion.

First-Person Perspective:
"Our building is owned by 1,400 people on three continents. Most never visit, and decisions are made by a vote in an app. Sometimes we don't even know a rule has changed until it impacts us. I wish there was a way for tenants to have a real say, not just be the product."
— Stefan, Tenant in a Tokenized Berlin Property

---

4. Transparency as Foundation, Not Feature

In traditional real estate, transparency is hard-won: hidden debts, shell companies, and off-balance-sheet financing abound. Tokenization promises transparency—every transaction on the chain, every vote, every dividend. Yet, too often, the promise is not realized. Offerings may tout 'full transparency' while publishing only selective dashboards or hiding key data behind complex, unaudited smart contracts.

True transparency requires much more:

- **Complete financial disclosure:** All cash flows, capital expenditures, rental income, debt service, and management fees should be reported on-chain and visible to all token holders.

- **Token use of proceeds:** Investors must be able to trace exactly where their money goes—acquisition, renovation, dividends, management, legal costs.
- **Historical context:** Past performance, prior ownership, and legal encumbrances (e.g., liens, disputes) must be documented, not buried.
- **Governance record:** Every governance decision, from rent policy to capital improvements, must be logged, timestamped, and open for audit.

Global Perspective:

Transparency is especially vital where traditional systems have failed. In Nigeria, tokenized land projects have helped reduce fraud by making title transfers public and traceable. In contrast, projects in parts of Eastern Europe have drawn scrutiny for using tokens to mask ownership changes and avoid local taxes.

Historical Analogy:

The rise of public REITs (Real Estate Investment Trusts) in the United States in the 1960s transformed real estate from a clubby, opaque world to a public, regulated, and relatively transparent asset class. The most successful REITs won investor trust by publishing audited financials, regular disclosures, and governance frameworks. Standards that tokenized real estate must now emulate and exceed.

---

5. Structuring Property Tokens for Ethics and Resilience

Not all property tokens are created equal. The choices made at the structuring phase—rights, risk allocation, governance, compliance—define not only the platform's viability, but its moral legitimacy.

High-Risk Structures (and Their Pitfalls)

- **Pseudo-securities:** Platforms that mimic securities: paying dividends or sharing profits, but avoid registration, leaving investors unprotected and markets unstable.

- **Opaque pooling:** Multiple properties bundled with little or no disclosure of individual asset performance or risk, making due diligence impossible.
- **Tokens on disputed or distressed titles:** Fast-tracking tokenization of assets with legal clouds—foreclosures, unpaid taxes, unresolved disputes—invites disaster for investors and communities alike.

First-Person Account:
"I invested in a tokenized apartment pool. Six months later, I learned one property was tied up in a court case. My tokens became worthless overnight. No warning, no recourse."
— Raj, Investor, Singapore

Ethically Aligned Structures

- **Reg D, Reg CF, or Reg A+ compliant tokens:** Clear, legal investor protections—disclosures, recourse, suitability checks, and limitations on non-accredited participation.
- **Token-holder rights and constraints:** Explicit limits on absentee ownership, with voting rights adjusted to protect tenants and local communities.
- **Community and equity set-asides:** Mandating a share of tokens be held by residents, local organizations, or nonprofits to anchor investment in place.

Industry Spotlight:

A U.S.-based platform, HomeStake, structured its tokens as SEC-registered securities, included tenant veto rights on certain property decisions, and reserved 10% of tokens for community land trusts. Returns were lower than 'high-flying' platforms, but tenant retention, local support, and long-term investor confidence were far higher.

Compliance Is the Floor, Not the Ceiling

Attempting to evade regulation under the flag of 'decentralization' is a recipe for ethical and legal disaster. The regulatory perimeter is moving outward; the SEC, ESMA, MAS, and others are expanding their scrutiny to cover nearly all tokenized property offerings. Platforms that lead on compliance, transparency, and governance will not only avoid the "Wild West" backlash but will set the bar for the next generation.

---

6. Tokenization and Community Impact: Beyond Profit and Extraction

Every tokenized property sits within a real neighborhood. The impact of digital ownership on real places is profound, often overlooked, and fraught with risk.

Speculation and Displacement

If property tokens are marketed mainly to global investors with no connection to the local area, the risk of speculative buying and rapid flipping rises. This can:

- Drive up rents and property values, pricing out longtime residents.
- Incentivize conversions to short-term rentals, hollowing out community cohesion.
- Shift governance away from those most affected by property decisions.

Environmental and Land Use Ethics

Tokenization brings the possibility of algorithmic, globalized decision-making to local land use. Without ethical guardrails, this could:

- Prioritize short-term profit (e.g., rapid renovation, Airbnb conversions) over environmental sustainability.
- Encourage overdevelopment, neglecting green space and long-term resilience.
- Undermine historic preservation or local culture, replacing stewardship with extraction.

Case Study:

A Brazilian favela tokenization project intended to 'unlock value' for residents. However, after token sales were opened globally, speculators quickly outbid locals. Within a year, evictions increased, and communal spaces were privatized. The backlash forced the platform to retool: now, only verified local residents can hold majority tokens, and a portion of **profits funds community development.**

Positive Models: Building Inclusive Wealth

- **Resident-first token offerings:** Tenants and community members are offered tokens at preferential rates before outside investors.
- **Land trust partnerships:** A share of tokens is held in trust, guaranteeing permanent affordability or community benefit.
- **Profit-sharing for local impact:** A set percentage of rental income or appreciation flows to neighborhood projects: schools, infrastructure, or social enterprises.

Global Perspective:
In South Africa, a project called "Ubuntu Tokens" linked urban renewal to social equity by requiring every tokenized property to allocate 20% of tokens to a local cooperative, with dividends funding education and health services.

---

7. Redefining Value: From Scarcity to Stewardship

The traditional model of real estate rests on scarcity—land is fixed—so those who own, win. This model incentivizes hoarding, speculation, and cycles of boom and bust.

Tokenization, by contrast, has the potential to shift the paradigm toward **stewardship**, shared ownership, aligned incentives, and long-term investment in place, only if designed with intention.

Aligning Token Flows with Long-Term Value

- **Sustainability over speculation:** Tokenomics can be structured to reward long-term holding, green building, and social impact, not just quick trading.
- **Absentee ownership limits:** Placing caps on the percentage of tokens any one party (especially anonymous wallets) can hold, or requiring physical presence or community engagement for major decisions.
- **Governance overlays:** Embedding local input, public oversight, and legal accountability into every decision, so that digital owners

remain grounded in real-world responsibilities.

Historical Analogy: The Community Land Trust

The community land trust movement, which began in the 1960s' U.S. civil rights era, offers a blueprint. By separating land ownership from building ownership and placing land in trust for perpetual affordability, CLTs have stabilized neighborhoods, empowered residents, and resisted gentrification. Tokenization, if ethically structured, can scale this model, making stewardship, not speculation, the default.

---

8. Legal and Regulatory Obligations: The Maturing of the Market

Most tokenized real estate offerings qualify as securities under U.S. and global law. This reality cannot be dodged with the 'decentralization' rhetoric or creative structuring. Ethical platforms must lead, not lag, on compliance.

Legal Frameworks to Observe

- **SEC Registration or Exemption:** Most token offerings require Reg D, Reg A+, or Reg CF filings—disclosures, audited financials, investor thresholds, and anti-fraud measures.
- **Accurate Disclosures:** Every risk, encumbrance, financial detail, and governance rule must be clearly spelled out.
- **Cross-border compliance:** If tokens are offered globally, platforms must align with MiCA (EU), SFC (Hong Kong), MAS (Singapore), and FATF standards.

Consequences of Noncompliance

Platforms that skirt these obligations not only risk enforcement action: shutting down, fines, clawbacks, but also destroy trust in the very model of tokenized real estate. Legal compliance is the baseline for legitimacy.

First-Person Account:

"We launched our first token project, thinking we could stay under the SEC radar by selling only to 'members.' After a year, we faced an

investigation and had to buy back every token. It cost us everything. Now we're registered, transparent, and building back trust—slowly."
— Chris, Real Estate Token Founder

---

9. Global Perspectives: Tokenization Across Continents

Asia: Scaling Urban Inclusion

In Singapore, government-backed pilots use blockchain to fractionalize public housing, with built-in protections for low-income buyers and strict rules against speculation. In India, startups are using tokens to help slum dwellers secure legal title and access micro-mortgages, transforming informal land into a source of stability.

Africa: Land Rights and Restitution

In Kenya, tokenization projects are linking mobile money with blockchain land registries, allowing smallholder farmers to access credit and prove ownership in disputes, strengthening rural economies and resisting land grabs.

Middle East: Ownership and Sharia

Dubai and Abu Dhabi have explored "Sharia-compliant" real estate tokens, ensuring profit-sharing, local community engagement, and prohibition of speculation. Governance boards include local religious and community leaders to balance profit and ethical purpose.

Europe: Tenant Power in the Age of Tokens

Berlin, Stockholm, and Barcelona have seen strong tenants' unions demand—and sometimes win—guaranteed representation in tokenized property DAOs, ensuring that local voices are not drowned out by absentee investors.

Latin America: Resilience Amid Crisis

In Argentina and Venezuela, tokenization is used by local cooperatives to resist hyperinflation and property confiscation, but only when paired with community governance and anti-speculation limits.

---

10. Industry Spotlights: Innovation With Integrity

Case: SmartBlock, United States

SmartBlock launched a suite of tokenized REITs, each registered with the SEC and featuring quarterly audits, mandatory community engagement, and sustainability metrics. Investors receive both financial and "impact" dividends, with community representatives voting on capital allocations. Properties in gentrifying neighborhoods include buy-back rights for tenants and enforce local hiring for renovations.

Case: BlockCasa, Spain

BlockCasa focuses on small-town revitalization, allowing residents to co-invest alongside global capital. All tokenized assets require majority local approval for major decisions, and 15% of all profits are reinvested in local infrastructure. Tenants have a guaranteed option to buy in, and tokens are non-transferable for 24 months post-acquisition.

---

11. Redefining Success: From Market Returns to Social Impact

Ultimately, the success of tokenized real estate will not be measured solely by APYs, trading volumes, or total value locked. Its true legacy will be written in:

- The stability and affordability of neighborhoods.
- The empowerment of residents as owners, not just renters.
- The resilience of communities against speculation and displacement.
- The transparency and accountability of property markets.
- The ability of the model to withstand scrutiny from both investors and the public.

First-Person Account:

"Our neighborhood in Detroit was written off by investors for years. When we tokenized the block, we made sure every tenant could own a piece. Now, we're building not just wealth, but a future for our families. We have a say, and that changes everything."

— Keisha, Resident and Community Leader

12. Conclusion: Housing as a Human Right, Even on Chain

The digitization of real estate is not just a technical leap; it is a profound test of values. We are uploading the oldest assets of civilization onto the newest rails of technology. In the process, we must remember that **housing is not just a yield instrument; it is a foundation for life, security,** and **dignity.**

Ethical tokenization means:

- Refusing to reduce homes to code and communities to markets.
- Embedding participation, transparency, and stewardship into every contract.
- Recognizing that legal compliance, community impact, and user protection are not constraints, but prerequisites for legitimacy.
- Designing for the long-term health of people and places, not just for financial engineering.

Done right, tokenized real estate can break the cycle of exclusion, unlock new avenues for wealth-building, and make property markets more accountable, transparent, and just. Done wrong, it risks repeating—and amplifying—the mistakes of the past.

We are at a crossroads. The choice is not only technical or financial; it is, fundamentally, ethical. As founders, investors, policymakers, and citizens, it is ours to make. Let us choose wisely.

Chapter 5: Compliance Without Compromise: Navigating Global Law Ethically

Summary

In the decentralized age, law and code are often perceived as adversaries. Builders prize innovation and speed. Regulators emphasize structure and protection. But this dichotomy is false—and dangerous.

To scale responsibly, blockchain platforms must **embrace compliance as an ethical design principle**, not a post-launch problem. Regulation is not the enemy of innovation, it is the framework that sustains trust, unlocks institutional adoption, and prevents systemic harm.

This chapter explores how ethical alignment with **U.S. and international securities laws** strengthens credibility, protects users, and ensures long-term viability for DeFi and tokenized real estate platforms.

The Fallacy of "Decentralization as Immunity"

Some founders believe decentralization shields them from regulatory jurisdiction. However, courts and regulators increasingly recognize that:

- Code is authored by humans.
- Protocols are maintained by teams.
- Tokens, if sold with profit expectations, are **securities** under U.S. law.

Claiming decentralization does not absolve platforms of responsibility. In fact, the more economic power a protocol wields, the greater its ethical obligation to **align with the law, even when that law is imperfect or evolving.**

Understanding the Global Regulatory Landscape

United States – SEC & FINRA

- **The Howey Test** classifies any offering as a security if there's an investment of money in a common enterprise with an expectation of profit from the efforts of others.

- Tokenized real estate often qualifies under Reg D, Reg CF, or Reg A+ exemptions.
- KYC/AML obligations under the **Bank Secrecy Act** apply to custodians, marketplaces, and broker-dealers.
- Misleading disclosures or token marketing can trigger **Section 5 violations** and enforcement actions.

European Union – MiCA (Markets in Crypto-Assets)

- Requires whitepapers, stablecoin reserve disclosures, and conduct standards for issuers.
- Includes licensing and custody standards for service providers.
- Supports clear definitions of utility tokens, asset-referenced tokens, and e-money tokens.

Global Standards

- **FATF Travel Rule** for KYC/AML transparency across jurisdictions.
- **OECD Crypto-Asset Reporting Framework** for tax compliance.
- **Asia-Pacific** (e.g., Singapore, Japan): Progressive but increasingly stringent licensing regimes.

Ethics in Compliance: A Higher Standard

Legal minimums are **not enough** for platforms that wish to lead ethically. Going beyond compliance includes:

- Voluntary audits of smart contracts and custody infrastructure.
- Publishing **token holder rights**, dispute resolution paths, and liquidation protocols.
- Disclosing risks in **plain language**, not hidden in dense legal appendices.
- Offering **opt-in data privacy settings** aligned with GDPR and CCPA.

Regulators reward transparency. Investors reward trust. Ethics drives both.

Avoiding Common Compliance Failures (and Ethical Breaches)

1. **"Utility Token" Misclassification**
   Mislabeling a security token to avoid regulation is unethical. If investors expect returns, treat it as a security, offering full disclosures.
2. **No AML/KYC Enforcement**
   Platforms that allow anonymous capital flow, risk laundering and sanctions violations. Ethical platforms **verify identity while protecting privacy**.
3. **Custodial Mismanagement**
   If the platform holds assets, it holds responsibility. Lack of separation between user funds and platform operating capital is a breach of trust and regulation.
4. **Cross-Border Token Sales Without Jurisdictional Control**
   Issuing real estate tokens globally without localized compliance triggers **multi-country violations** and exposes users to legal uncertainty.

Tools for Ethical Global Compliance

1. **Compliance-as-a-Service APIs** – Embed KYC/AML, identity verification, and blacklist screening in real time.
2. **Regulatory Composable Layers** – Launch tokens with optional Reg D or Reg CF wrappers depending on geography.
3. **Legal Disclosures Engine** – Auto-generate disclosures based on asset type, risk profile, and jurisdiction.
4. **Modular Licensing** – Partner with licensed custodians and marketplaces to legally offer services in restricted zones.

Compliance no longer has to be expensive or slow. Modern compliance tools can be **modular, embedded, and scalable**.

Proactive Engagement with Regulators

Ethical platforms should not wait for subpoenas. They should **engage, educate, and evolve** alongside regulators:

- Publish open letters explaining protocol ethics and safeguards.
- Invite third-party legal scholars to review token structures.

- Collaborate with oversight bodies on pilot programs or sandbox environments.
- Contribute to public policy through transparent participation, not lobbying alone.

This collaborative posture **elevates your platform above the noise** and signals serious long-term intent.

Conclusion: Compliance Is the Foundation of Credibility

Ethical builders do not fear the law—they shape the future with it. In the age of tokenized capital and decentralized ownership, compliance is not a cost center, but **a competitive advantage**.

The innovators who survive regulatory scrutiny are those who align legal structure with ethical clarity; who code with compliance in mind; who treat investor protection as a brand promise, not a burden.

The question is no longer: "Can we avoid regulation?"
The question is: **"Can we become the model the world regulates toward?"**

Chapter 5: Expansion

---

1. Introduction: Law, Trust, and the New Digital Order

Every financial revolution faces a reckoning with the law. In the age of blockchain, tokenization, and borderless platforms, the rules of engagement are being rewritten not just by lawmakers and regulators, but by the very builders and investors who shape the new landscape. The challenge—and opportunity—is not to evade regulation, but to make compliance an asset: a source of trust, transparency, and ethical legitimacy.

For too long, innovators in blockchain and DeFi have regarded law and code as adversaries: one dynamic, the other static; one disruptive, the other conservative. But this false dichotomy has led to a cycle of hype, regulatory backlash, and user harm. Ethical platforms understand that compliance is not the enemy of innovation; it is the bedrock that enables real, durable change.

This chapter explores how global legal alignment, ethical clarity, and compliance-by-design can turn regulatory rigor from a constraint into a competitive advantage, anchoring tokenized real estate and DeFi platforms in credibility, longevity, and institutional acceptance.

---

2. The Myth of Decentralization as Immunity

The rallying cry of the blockchain era has been "decentralization," the notion that code, not corporations, can govern capital; that distributed ledgers can bypass borders, authorities, and gatekeepers. But the practical reality is more complex, and the legal risks more acute.

First-Person Account:
"As an early Ethereum developer, I believed that smart contracts could operate above the law. But when our protocol was exploited, and users lost millions, we realized regulators saw us—not the code—as responsible. Decentralization wasn't a shield. It was a call to ethical stewardship."
— Gavin, Protocol Co-Founder

Why "Decentralized" Doesn't Mean Unregulated

Regulators worldwide now recognize that code is written by humans, maintained by teams, and directed—whether directly or indirectly—by organizations or DAOs. The idea that mere distribution of servers, multisig wallets, or DAOs confers legal immunity has been debunked by courts in the United States, the European Union, and the Asia-Pacific.

When a platform sells tokens promising profit, coordinates upgrades, collects fees, or guides community decisions, it functions as an issuer. In the eyes of the law, **economic power creates ethical and legal responsibility**, even when protocols are 'governed' by code.

Case Law and Precedent

- **SEC v. Telegram**: The U.S. SEC halted the $1.7B-Gram token sale, arguing that distributed tokens with an expectation of profit from the efforts of others are securities, even when "decentralized" post-launch.
- **Commodity Futures Trading Commission v. Ooki DAO**: U.S. regulators served notice to DAO governance participants for alleged derivatives violations, signaling that decentralized

governance is no shield from enforcement.

These cases highlight a crucial truth: Regulatory frameworks will pursue those who control, promote, or benefit from protocols, not just those who formally 'own' them. The ethical lesson: With decentralization comes not just distributed power, but distributed duty.

---

3. The Global Regulatory Landscape: An Evolving Map

United States: SEC, FINRA, and the Howey Test

The U.S. is the world's deepest capital market—and the world's most litigious. U.S. securities law hinges on the **Howey Test**, which classifies any investment as a security if there is an investment of money in a common enterprise, with a reasonable expectation of profits derived from the efforts of others. Tokenized real estate, utility tokens with profit potential, and many DeFi instruments routinely meet these criteria.

- Exemptions and Pathways:
    - *Regulation D*: Allows private placements with accredited investors, requiring disclosure and filing but not public registration.
    - *Regulation A+*: Permits mini-IPOs, opening offerings to non-accredited investors with SEC review and ongoing reporting.
    - *Regulation Crowdfunding (Reg CF)*: Enables small-dollar investments with strict limits and intermediary requirements.

All pathways demand **Know Your Customer (KYC)** and **Anti-Money Laundering (AML)** checks per the Bank Secrecy Act. Violations can trigger criminal prosecution, fines, and civil suits.

- **FINRA** enforces standards for broker-dealers and tokenized securities marketplaces, focusing on clear disclosures, suitability, fair dealing, and investor communications.
- **Key Compliance Risks:**
    - Misleading token marketing (Section 5 violations)
    - Opaque disclosures or omitted risk factors
    - Custodial mismanagement (mixing user assets with

    - operating funds)
    - Cross-border token sales without jurisdictional controls

European Union: MiCA and Beyond

The EU's **Markets in Crypto-Assets (MiCA)** regulation sets a high bar for crypto offerings:

- Requires *whitepapers* detailing tokenomics, risks, and issuer identity.
- Demands *reserve disclosures* for stablecoins and asset-referenced tokens.
- Mandates *licensing* for service providers (wallets, exchanges, custodians).
- Enforces strict conduct standards—transparency, best execution, consumer protections.

MiCA is coupled with existing GDPR privacy law and anti-money laundering directives (AMLD5 and 6).

Asia-Pacific: Innovation meets Regulation

- **Singapore's MAS (Monetary Authority of Singapore)**: Operates a licensing regime for digital payment token services, demanding AML/CFT compliance, technological due diligence, and ongoing supervision.
- **Japan's FSA**: Requires crypto exchanges to register, hold capital reserves, segregate client assets, and comply with annual audits.

Global Standards: FATF, OECD, and Multilateral Protocols

- **FATF (Financial Action Task Force)**: Implements the Travel Rule for KYC/AML information across jurisdictions.
- **OECD**: Introduces the Crypto-Asset Reporting Framework (CARF) for tax compliance, mandating automatic exchange of information about crypto asset holders.
- **Cross-border Reality**: Platforms must now address overlapping, sometimes conflicting regimes, and ethical leadership means building above the minimum bar.

---

4. Ethics in Compliance: Raising the Standard

Legal compliance sets the floor; ethics sets the ceiling. The most resilient, respected platforms understand that surviving in a post-regulatory world means going **beyond the letter of the law**.

Voluntary Audits and Transparency

Ethical platforms commission independent, third-party audits of smart contracts, custody processes, governance systems, and security infrastructure. They publish the results in plain language, not as a marketing ploy, but as a mark of genuine accountability.

Industry Example:
A U.S. tokenized REIT not only files required SEC disclosures but posts full protocol audits, asset-level breakdowns, and risk matrices online. Investors can review every aspect—code, contracts, and capital flows—before participating.

User Rights and Dispute Resolution

Instead of burying rights in dense legal appendices, leading platforms create **public, readable summaries** of investor rights, paths to dispute resolution, and liquidation protocols. For complex DeFi products, simulated "stress scenarios" are provided in the onboarding process, enabling users to see the real consequences of black swan events.

Privacy by Design

GDPR and CCPA are the legal minimums. Ethical platforms give users opt-in, granular control over data use, with privacy settings embedded in onboarding, not hidden in fine print. Sensitive information is encrypted, access is monitored, and retention is minimized.

First-Person Account:
"I used to worry about sharing my ID for KYC. But when a platform explained how my data is stored, how long, and who can access it—and let me opt out of nonessential sharing—I felt respected, not just processed."
— Lucas, Investor, Portugal

Proactive Risk Disclosure

Ethical compliance means **disclosing risks in plain language**: explaining market volatility, liquidity limits, redemption lockups, protocol governance, and what happens in crisis, not just what happens in best-case scenarios.

---

5. Common Compliance Failures: Ethics on Trial

Regulatory enforcement often follows egregious ethical breaches, moments when the drive for scale or profit overrides caution, duty, and honesty.

a) Misclassification of 'Utility' Tokens

Labeling a profit-sharing token as a 'utility' to sidestep securities regulation is not innovation; it is deception. If investors expect returns, the token is a security. Anything less than full registration and disclosure is unethical and, increasingly, illegal.

Case Study:
A high-profile token platform in the U.S. sold millions of dollars of 'membership tokens' that gave holders rights to profit-sharing and governance. When enforcement arrived, the founders claimed 'utility.' The SEC disagreed. Investors faced losses, and the platform lost all trust.

b) Ignoring AML/KYC Obligations

Permitting anonymous capital flows—especially from sanctioned regions or with no source-of-funds verification—exposes platforms to money laundering, terrorist financing, and blacklisting. Ethical compliance means robust identity checks, without resorting to data overcollection or discriminatory profiling.

First-Person Perspective:
"I lost money on a project that got shut down for laundering. No one ever checked my identity, and the founders disappeared with the funds. If I'd seen KYC, I would have trusted the platform—and regulators did, too."
— Adisa, Investor, Kenya

c) Custodial Mismanagement

Commingling user assets with platform operating funds or failing to segregate accounts are both regulatory violations and ethical failures. When protocols collapse or are hacked, user funds are often unrecoverable.

Industry Example:
The 2022 FTX collapse highlighted catastrophic failures in asset segregation. Billions in user funds were lost, and the industry's credibility suffered. Platforms that segregated funds, maintained regular audits, and published cold wallet addresses retained user trust and survived the fallout.

d) Cross-Border Token Sales Without Jurisdictional Compliance

Selling tokens globally, without country-specific compliance checks, exposes platforms to regulatory whiplash: sudden bans, asset freezes, lawsuits, and criminal exposure for founders and investors alike.

Case Study:
A European property token project marketed shares to U.S. and Chinese investors without proper exemptions or filings. Both countries banned the tokens, freezing secondary markets and triggering lawsuits. Investors faced uncertainty and loss.

---

5. Tools and Tactics for Ethical Compliance: From Burden to Asset

Modern compliance need not be slow, expensive, or stifling. New technologies and best practices make ethical alignment scalable and seamless.

a) Compliance-as-a-Service APIs

Platforms can now integrate real-time KYC/AML checks, blacklist screening, sanctions filters, and identity verification using plug-and-play APIs. These tools enable platforms to onboard users globally, while respecting local requirements.

b) Regulatory Composable Layers

Smart token platforms launch assets with modular compliance wrappers: Reg D for accredited U.S. investors, Reg S for non-U.S. holders, Reg CF for crowdfunding. Tokens are dynamically geofenced and rights-adjusted depending on user jurisdiction.

c) Legal Disclosure Engines

Automated disclosure generators create clear, readable, and jurisdiction-specific risk and rights statements for every asset, based on asset type, investor profile, and geography. These are surfaced in user onboarding and updated as regulations evolve.

d) Modular Licensing and Partnerships

Rather than building compliance infrastructure from scratch, ethical platforms partner with licensed custodians, broker-dealers, or exchanges. Services are "white-labeled" and embedded, enabling compliant offerings even in highly regulated markets.

Industry Spotlight:
A leading real estate tokenization platform in Singapore uses a hybrid compliance stack: MAS-licensed custody, third-party KYC API, and smart contract audits. The result: fast onboarding, zero enforcement actions, and institutional-grade credibility.

---

6. Proactive Engagement: Collaborating With Regulators

The most successful platforms do not wait for subpoenas or enforcement actions. They actively engage with regulators, legal scholars, and oversight bodies from the earliest design stages.

a) Open Dialogue

Ethical platforms publish open letters, technical whitepapers, and impact assessments explaining how protocols align with both the spirit and letter of existing law. They invite scrutiny, answer questions, and correct misconceptions in real time.

b) External Legal Review

Rather than relying solely on in-house counsel, platforms invite third-party experts to review token structures, governance models, and compliance mechanisms. These reviews are published with summaries for non-lawyers.

c) Participation in Regulatory Sandboxes

By joining government-sponsored sandboxes or pilot programs, platforms demonstrate a willingness to test, iterate, and improve within regulatory frameworks, gaining early trust and feedback.

d) Contributing to Public Policy

Serious innovators shape the rules of the road by collaborating in public forums, submitting commentary, or joining industry groups. They advocate for pragmatic, innovation-friendly regulations backed by transparent data and ethical arguments, not just lobbying dollars.

First-Person Account:
"We joined the Singapore MAS sandbox because we wanted to build with feedback—not after enforcement. That partnership accelerated our growth and established us as a trusted brand, not just another token."
— Priya, Head of Compliance, FinTech Startup

---

7. Global Perspectives: Compliance Culture in Context

United States: Litigation, Enforcement, and Precedent

The U.S. remains the gold standard for legal clarity; every rule is tested in court, and every enforcement creates a new doctrine. Surviving here requires overcompliance, not minimalism.

Europe: Data and Consumer Protection

The EU's culture of user privacy, data rights, and consumer empowerment means platforms must prioritize transparency, opt-in consent, and robust dispute resolution.

Asia: Innovation-Forward, Caution-Driven

Singapore, Hong Kong, and Japan balance rapid fintech growth with strict licensing, AML, and ongoing supervision. Platforms here are rewarded for transparency, resilience, and proactive regulator engagement.

Africa: Opportunity and Trust

Emerging markets in Africa see compliance as a path to attracting institutional investment and user trust, especially for land rights, microfinance, and mobile money platforms.

Latin America: Regulatory Uncertainty and Grassroots Ethics

With fast-moving crypto adoption but uneven law, platforms in Latin America often self-regulate, building compliance and consumer protection into UX as a shield against market volatility and state crackdowns.

---

8. Historical Analogies: Compliance as a Competitive Moat

The Rise of Modern Banking

The early 20th-century banking industry was a Wild West of panics, failures, and lost deposits. The creation of the Federal Reserve, FDIC, and state banking commissions—along with strict compliance rules—transformed banking from a confidence game to a trusted backbone of the economy.

The Dot-Com Crash and Sarbanes-Oxley

After the dot-com bubble burst in 2000, the Sarbanes-Oxley Act imposed rigorous disclosure, accounting, and internal controls on public companies. At first decried as stifling, SOX ultimately restored trust and drew trillions back into the market. The most resilient tech firms embedded compliance into their DNA.

The Emergence of ESG and Impact Investing

Today's investors reward not just compliance, but ethical leadership. The rise of environmental, social, and governance (ESG) standards—often going beyond legal mandates—demonstrates that ethical alignment drives both market value and social impact.

9. Investor and User Perspectives: Compliance as Value Proposition

Tina, Institutional Investor, London:
"We will not touch platforms that treat compliance as an afterthought. Our LPs demand audit trails, clear risk reporting, and legal clarity. The platforms that survive our diligence process are the ones that make compliance visible, measurable, and embedded."

Jorge, Retail User, Mexico City:
"I used to jump into new tokens for the hype. But after losing money on a noncompliant project, I look for badges, licenses, and published audits. If a platform doesn't show its compliance, I don't invest—no matter the returns."

---

10. The Business Case: Compliance as a Competitive Advantage

Ethical compliance is not a cost center; it is a catalyst for:

- **Institutional adoption:** Pension funds, banks, and family offices only partner with compliant, transparent platforms.
- **User retention:** Users stay when they feel protected by clear rules, fair recourse, and privacy.
- **Resilience to shocks:** Platforms that withstand enforcement, market crashes, or hacks are those with robust compliance and contingency plans.
- **Brand value:** In an industry rife with fraud and collapse, trust is the rarest and most defensible asset.

---

11. Conclusion: Toward a New Model of Compliance and Innovation

The innovators who will lead the next decade are not those who evade regulation, but those who **shape it**. By aligning legal structure with ethical clarity, by coding compliance into every contract, and by making investor protection a living brand promise, blockchain and DeFi builders can create platforms that endure, scale, and transform markets responsibly.

The question for every founder, developer, and investor is not "How do we avoid regulation?" but **"How do we become the example the world regulates toward?"**

Compliance is not a box to check. It is the foundation of trust and the future of the industry.

Chapter 6: The Fair DAO: Governance, Voting, and Community Justice

Summary

In a decentralized world, governance is power. Who decides how a protocol evolves, how funds are used, or how disputes are resolved? In traditional finance, that power is centralized—boards, executives, and regulators. In blockchain, it is distributed through **DAOs**—Decentralized Autonomous Organizations.

But decentralization alone does not ensure fairness. In fact, without intentional ethical design, DAOs can replicate the same injustices they were created to eliminate: **centralized power, disenfranchisement, insider dominance, and lack of accountability.**

This chapter explores how to build DAOs that are not only technically sound but ethically fair, socially representative, and legally sustainable.

The Illusion of Democratic Governance

Many DAOs operate on the principle of *1 token = 1 vote*. On the surface, this seems democratic. But in practice, it often means:

- Whales dominate proposals.
- Token-rich insiders influence outcomes.
- Voter apathy and complexity exclude smaller holders.
- No legal accountability exists for governance decisions.

In short: plutocracy masquerading as democracy.

To create ethical DAOs, we must move from token-weighted governance toward stakeholder-balanced models, where voice is not solely determined by capital.

Principles of Ethical DAO Governance

1. **Inclusivity**
   Governance participation must be accessible across education levels, languages, and tech familiarity. This includes:
   - Intuitive interfaces.
   - Multilingual voting instructions.
   - Mobile-first access for low-bandwidth users.
2. **Transparency**
   All proposals, votes, and outcomes should be recorded, searchable, and verifiable on-chain. Shadow voting, pre-loaded outcomes, or insider coordination must be exposed.
3. **Proportionality**
   Not every decision should require the same weight. Ethical DAOs should tier governance:
   - **Operational** decisions via core team or delegates.
   - **Strategic** decisions via full token holder vote.
   - **Constitutional** changes via supermajority or multi-stakeholder consensus.
4. **Deliberation**
   Voting should not be rushed. Ethical DAOs allow time for:
   - Community debate.
   - Public audits of proposals.
   - Independent analysis and risk assessment.

DAO Failures and Their Lessons

Several DAO collapses have revealed ethical blind spots:

- **The DAO (2016):** A flaw in smart contract logic allowed a $60M hack. Governance was powerless to respond without Ethereum's hard fork, raising questions about immutability vs. justice.

- **Maker DAO:** Centralized actors were often more influential than the distributed community, leading to concerns over protocol capture.
- **Fei Protocol:** An over-engineered system created price instability—despite good intentions—highlighting the risk of complexity without user input.

Ethical DAOs learn from these failures—not by avoiding risk, but by building systems that adapt transparently, respond collectively, and embed responsibility.

Ethical Voting Models: Beyond Capital-Weighted Systems

To promote fairness, DAOs can explore:

- **Quadratic Voting** – Reduces the influence of whales by making each additional vote cost exponentially more tokens.
- **Reputation-Based Voting** – Rewards long-term contributors, not just capital providers.
- **Time-Weighted Staking** – Gives more voice to those who stake tokens longer, discouraging flash voting.
- **Multi-Stakeholder DAOs** – Split governance among token holders, platform users, and external validators (e.g., legal or civic reps).

These models aren't perfect, but they move us closer to **governance by values, not just wallets.**

Dispute Resolution and Community Justice

DAOs must prepare for disagreement. Ethical governance demands:

- **On-chain dispute processes**, such as Aragon Court or Kleros.
- **Delegated mediators** or rotating juries for low-stakes issues.
- **Clear escalation paths** for high-impact conflicts.
- **Human-readable constitutions** outlining DAO responsibilities, rights, and remedy options.

Code is deterministic. Life is not. DAOs must leave space for context, fairness, and redemption.

Legal Recognition and DAO Wrappers

To bridge the gap between code and law, DAOs can adopt legal wrappers such as:

- **Wyoming DAO LLC** (United States).
- **UNA structures** (Marshall Islands).
- **Private limited DAOs** (Switzerland, Singapore).

These wrappers help:

- Limit personal liability.
- Enter contracts with vendors or regulators.
- Hold real-world assets.
- Prove compliance in tokenized property or securities offerings.

Ethical DAOs protect not only their users but also their builders and communities through a proper legal structure.

The Future: Regenerative Governance

The next generation of DAOs won't just vote. They will:

- Evolve based on performance data.
- Use AI-assisted proposal analysis.
- Incorporate ethics councils.
- Self-audit for concentration and capture risks.

The goal isn't just decentralization. The goal is **regeneration**—systems that reward collaboration, adapt to complexity, and align incentives for the long term.

Conclusion: Building the Infrastructure of Collective Intelligence

DAO governance is not a product. It's a process.

To get it right, we must replace the obsession with token price and protocol control with a deeper commitment: to fairness, voice, transparency, and adaptability. Ethical governance means everyone matters—**even those with less to vote, but more to lose.**

The fair DAO isn't easy to build. But it is worth building. It is how we honor the decentralized future we claim to believe in.

Chapter 6: Expansion

---

1. Introduction: The New Arena of Power

The invention of the DAO (Decentralized Autonomous Organization) was hailed as a revolution not just in technology, but in governance. For the first time, human communities could coordinate, vote, and allocate resources at a global scale, all without a central administrator. By encoding rules into smart contracts and opening participation to anyone with a token and an internet connection, DAOs promised to deliver what corporations, cooperatives, and governments have long struggled to achieve: truly democratic, transparent, and fair decision-making.

Yet, as DAOs proliferated across DeFi, tokenized real estate, gaming, and beyond, it became clear that decentralization alone is no guarantee of justice. Without careful, ethical design, DAOs can amplify the very harms—centralized power, exclusion, insider dominance, and unaccountable decision-making—they were created to solve.

This chapter explores how the infrastructure of collective intelligence can be built for **fairness**. It examines the technical, social, and ethical dimensions of DAO governance, drawing on industry lessons, historical context, first-person accounts, and a global lens. The aim: Not just to create decentralized protocols, but to engineer organizations that truly empower their communities, protect the vulnerable, and model justice for a digital age.

---

2. The Illusion of Democracy: When 1 Token = 1 Vote Becomes Plutocracy

Most DAOs begin with a simple principle: 1 token equals one vote. At first glance, this seems the height of democracy; every member gets a say, proportional to their stake. But as DAOs have grown and capital has concentrated, a sobering pattern has emerged. Large holders ("whales") increasingly dictate outcomes. Token-rich insiders propose, coordinate, and win votes, often behind closed channels. Meanwhile, smaller holders, newcomers, and non-technical participants face a landscape that is complex, intimidating, and ultimately exclusionary.

Industry Case: The Plutocracy Problem

Consider a DeFi protocol where governance is determined entirely by token holdings. During a critical vote to change fee structures, a handful of wallets—representing less than 1% of participants—controlled over 50% of votes. Their interests aligned: Maximizing short-term fees over long-term sustainability. The result? Rapid fee hikes, user attrition, and eventually, a forked protocol as disgruntled community members left to start anew.

First-Person Account

"I bought a few tokens and was excited to join the DAO. But when I tried to submit a proposal, it was buried before anyone saw it. Then, I watched the same few whales push through their agenda, over and over. It felt less like democracy, more like a club for the rich."
— Ada, DAO participant, Lagos

The Mechanisms of Exclusion

This pattern is not unique. Across dozens of DAOs, governance often falls prey to:

- Low participation from the majority ("governance apathy"), as the cost of voting (gas, research, time) outweighs perceived influence.
- Token accumulation and "vote buying" by insiders, venture funds, or exchanges, who then coordinate outcomes privately.
- Lack of accessibility, complex UIs, English-only documentation, high-tech barriers, and little support for low-bandwidth or mobile users.

In practice, **plutocracy masquerades as democracy**. This is not just a technical failure, but an ethical one, a violation of the principles DAOs were meant to enshrine.

---

3. Principles of Ethical DAO Governance

If DAOs are to fulfill their promise, governance must be engineered for fairness, not just efficiency. This requires moving beyond "one token, one vote" to embrace inclusivity, transparency, proportionality, deliberation, and adaptive justice.

a) Inclusivity: Voice Beyond Capital

Ethical DAOs are accessible to people across education, language, geography, and technological comfort. This means:

- **Intuitive interfaces**: Voting platforms must be usable for non-experts, with clear instructions, visual cues, and guided steps.
- **Multilingual support**: Proposals and ballots should be translated and localized for global communities.
- **Mobile-first access**: Many in emerging markets rely on phones and limited data. UIs must be light, fast, and functional on all devices.

First-Person Account

"I joined a DAO from my phone in the Philippines. The platform was heavy, slow, and only in English. I couldn't understand half the proposals, so I stopped voting. My friends had the same issue—we were included in theory, excluded in practice."
— Rey, Community Member

b) Transparency: Governance as a Public Ledger

True transparency means more than open-source code. Every proposal, debate, vote, and outcome must be **searchable, timestamped,** and **verifiable** on-chain. Shadow voting, preloaded outcomes, and insider coordination must be exposed to sunlight.

Ethical DAOs publish real-time dashboards of participation, voting patterns, and proposer histories. They flag suspicious coordination, disclose all conflicts of interest, and invite public audit.

c) Proportionality: Tiered and Responsive Decision-making

Ethical DAOs tier governance:

- **Operational decisions** (e.g., small grants, parameter tweaks): Delegated to working groups or core contributors, with regular community review.
- **Strategic decisions** (e.g., protocol upgrades, budget allocations): Voted on by the full tokenholder base, with minimum participation thresholds.

- **Constitutional changes** (e.g., governance model reforms, asset liquidation): Require supermajorities, time delays, and multi-stakeholder consensus (token holders, users, external validators).

d) Deliberation: Space for Debate and Revision

Voting is not enough. Ethical DAOs create time and tools for:

- **Community debate:** Dedicated forums, structured argumentation, and encouragement for dissenting voices.
- **Public audits:** Proposals are reviewed for technical, financial, and ethical risk by independent panels before voting.
- **Iteration and amendment:** Proposals can be revised in response to feedback, with clear windows for reconsideration.

Industry Spotlight:

In one global art DAO, each major proposal must go through a 14-day "deliberation window," including open Q&A, third-party risk assessment, and multilingual community calls. This slows decision-making, but increases legitimacy and engagement.

---

4. Lessons From DAO Failures: Immutability, Capture, and Complexity

DAOs are new, and their failures are instructive. Each high-profile collapse reveals both technical and ethical blind spots.

The DAO (2016): Immutability vs. Justice

The original DAO—an Ethereum-based investment fund—was famously hacked due to a smart contract bug. Governance was paralyzed; only a hard fork of Ethereum could reverse the exploit. The crisis sparked a philosophical war: Is code the final law, or should justice sometimes override immutability? The Ethereum community chose justice, but at the cost of chain unity and trust.

MakerDAO: Centralization by Any Other Name

As MakerDAO grew, a core group of large token holders and insiders began dominating governance. Critical changes—interest rates, collateral types—were often decided in private, and later ratified through "community" votes. This centralization led to accusations of protocol capture, even as Maker sought to expand inclusivity.

Fei Protocol: Complexity Without Consent

Fei Protocol's novel stabilization mechanism was well-intentioned, but so complex that few users understood it. When instability hit, governance tools failed to adapt quickly, as most community members lacked the technical insight to intervene.

The lesson: Complexity without education and consent is a risk to fairness.

---

5. Ethical Voting Models: Beyond Capital-Weighted Systems

To escape the plutocracy trap, DAOs are experimenting with alternative voting systems. These models aim to balance power, reward long-term contributors, and promote diverse perspectives.

Quadratic Voting

Each additional vote costs exponentially more tokens, reducing the dominance of whales and encouraging coalitions of smaller holders. Quadratic voting has been piloted in Gitcoin and several public goods DAOs, increasing diversity of outcomes and discouraging vote buying.

Reputation-based Voting

Power accrues to those who contribute over time—through code, support, education, or community building—not just to those with capital. Reputation points are earned, not bought, and decay if inactive. This model empowers doers and protects against flash-in-the-pan speculation.

Industry Example:
A leading DeFi protocol assigns "reputation multipliers" for users who participate in governance, propose successful improvements, or mentor new members. Over time, governance becomes less about wealth, more about stewardship.

Time-weighted Staking

The longer one's tokens are staked, the more weight their votes carry. This discourages opportunistic "flash voting" and rewards those with patience and alignment to long-term protocol health.

Multi-Stakeholder DAOs

Governance is split among multiple constituencies: token holders, users, external validators (e.g., legal or civic representatives), and community delegates. Each group has veto rights or weighted influence, forcing negotiation and coalition-building.

Real-World Analogy: Co-ops and Parliaments

Traditional co-ops, credit unions, and even parliaments employ similar multi-constituency governance, using checks, balances, and veto powers to prevent dominance by any one group. These analogies remind us that DAOs are not just code; they are social systems, inheriting lessons from centuries of organizational theory.

---

6. Dispute Resolution and Community Justice

No governance model is complete without robust mechanisms for resolving disagreement and redressing harm. The unique nature of DAOs—global, pseudonymous, and autonomous—demands new approaches to community justice.

On-Chain Dispute Mechanisms

Projects like Aragon Court and Kleros deploy blockchain juries—randomly selected, incentivized participants—to arbitrate low-stakes conflicts. Their verdicts are binding, transparent, and appealable, with "juror" pools rewarded for accurate, fair decisions.

Delegated Mediators and Rotating Juries

For routine disputes, DAOs can employ rotating panels of trusted delegates or peer mediators. These groups resolve issues quickly, freeing the community for major decisions.

Human-Readable Constitutions

Ethical DAOs codify their rights, responsibilities, and recourse options in plain language—"human-readable" constitutions—so all participants can understand the rules and remedies. When in doubt, justice favors the vulnerable, not just the efficient.

High-Impact Escalation Paths

For system-wide emergencies—hacks, protocol failures, etc—DAOs must have clear escalation: emergency councils, time-locked vetos, or even off-chain arbitration, when code cannot resolve the issue.

First-Person Account

"Our DAO was hit by a scam proposal. By the time we realized, funds were gone. Now, we have a two-step dispute system: First, a quick peer review, then a full community vote if needed. It slowed us down, but saved us from more damage."
— Xia, DAO Moderator, China

---

7. Legal Recognition and DAO Wrappers: Bridging Code and Law

As DAOs grow, they face the challenge of interacting with the "real world," signing contracts, holding assets, defending against lawsuits. Legal wrappers give DAOs a recognized identity, limit member liability, and enable compliant operations.

Global Legal Structures for DAOs

- **Wyoming DAO LLC (U.S.):** Grants DAOs limited liability, the ability to contract, and protection under state law.
- **UNA Structures (Marshall Islands):** Provides DAO legal personality, asset ownership, and global recognition.
- **Private Limited DAOs (Switzerland, Singapore):** Hybrid corporate/DAO forms that blend on-chain governance with off-chain legal compliance.

Why Legal Wrappers Matter

Legal recognition enables DAOs to:

- Limit personal risk for members and contributors.
- Enter contracts with vendors, investors, and regulators.
- Hold real-world assets (property, IP, fiat) in the name of the organization.
- Prove compliance in tokenized property, securities offerings, or labor law.

Industry Case:
A tokenized real estate DAO in Switzerland registered as a GmbH, allowing it to hold property deeds, sign service contracts, and resolve disputes under Swiss law. This hybrid model attracted institutional investors and enabled cross-border property management.

---

8. Community Stewardship: Designing for Social and Global Impact

The best DAOs do not measure success only by token price or protocol TVL, but by their **social impact**: inclusivity, community wealth, and lasting resilience.

Tokenization and Community DAOs

Tokenized real estate and other physical asset DAOs must recognize their impact on real people: tenants, workers, neighbors, and local governments. Ethical governance means embedding community voices and protections into decision-making.

- Community board seats or veto rights.
- Reserved tokens for local residents, nonprofits, or cooperatives.
- Transparent reporting on social and environmental impact.

Case Study: Community Wealth Building

In Detroit, a real estate DAO allocated 25% of tokens to local residents, with decisions on repairs and tenant policy subject to community vote. This structure stabilized rents, increased trust, and generated lasting neighborhood improvements.

Environmental and Labor Justice

DAOs with physical operations—mining, property, logistics—must account for their environmental footprint and labor practices. Governance can include sustainability mandates, worker representation, and public reporting on impact.

Global Perspective:
DAOs in Brazil, India, and Kenya increasingly build social charters pledging a share of profits for local education, healthcare, or green projects. These are not acts of charity, but investments in the long-term health of the ecosystem.

---

9. Regenerative Governance: AI, Ethics Councils, and Self-Audit

The next generation of DAOs will not merely decentralize; they will **regenerate**, evolving based on data, collective learning, and ethical review.

Adaptive Protocols

DAOs can use AI and analytics to detect voter concentration, participation decline, or governance manipulation. Automated alerts prompt reforms, audits, or community discussion.

Ethics Councils

Some DAOs form standing ethics committees, diverse panels tasked with reviewing major proposals for social impact, inclusion, and long-term risk. Their findings are published, debated, and can trigger mandatory reconsideration.

Self-Audit and Reflexivity

Mature DAOs embed regular self-audit cycles, measuring governance concentration, proposal diversity, and stakeholder satisfaction. They experiment with reforms—randomized voting, rotating leadership, public surveys—and publish results.

First-Person Account

"Every year, our DAO holds a governance audit. We look at who's voting,

who's being left out, and whether we're meeting our values. Last year, we added quadratic voting after seeing whales dominate. It wasn't perfect, but it made us more honest."
— Mateus, DAO Auditor, Brazil

---

10. Global Case Studies: DAOs in Context

Asia: DAOs for Financial Inclusion

In Vietnam and Indonesia, DAOs are being used to manage micro-loan pools for rural entrepreneurs. Governance is localized, with voting weighted toward borrower groups, ensuring capital serves community needs.

Africa: DAOs for Land Rights

Kenyan cooperatives are experimenting with DAOs to manage land titles and community farming. Decision-making includes elders, women's groups, and youth councils, balancing tradition and innovation.

Europe: Art and Culture DAOs

In Paris, an art DAO pools funds for emerging artists, with governance split among creators, collectors, and critics. Proposals for funding are debated in both online and live forums, and all votes are recorded on-chain for transparency.

North America: Regenerative Real Estate DAOs

Canadian DAOs focus on sustainable land management, with explicit environmental targets and community benefit agreements. Governance integrates indigenous voices and requires consensus for major land use changes.

Latin America: DAOs and Political Participation

Mexico City piloted a DAO for urban planning, enabling residents to propose, debate, and vote on local initiatives. Results showed increased trust, diverse participation, and new alliances across traditional divides.

---

11. The Future: Collective Intelligence as Ethical Infrastructure

DAOs are not just tools for voting or allocating capital; they are experiments in **collective intelligence**. The systems we design now—how we balance voice and value, transparency and privacy, efficiency and deliberation—will shape the next century of digital community.

Cultural Evolution and Ethical Ambition

As DAOs spread from finance to art, science, politics, and climate action, the stakes will rise. Building ethical governance is not a static task, but an ongoing process requiring humility, learning, and a willingness to evolve.

Historical Analogy: The Magna Carta of the Chain

Just as the Magna Carta limited the power of kings and seeded the rule of law, the first truly fair DAOs will set precedents—on rights, representation, and justice—that echo for generations. The protocols and charters we write today are the foundation of digital citizenship tomorrow.

---

12. Conclusion: Honoring the Promise of Decentralization

The dream of the DAO is a world where power is not hoarded, but shared; where decisions are not dictated, but deliberated; where justice is not imposed, but enacted by the community itself.

To build this future, we must go beyond the surface of decentralization, beyond token prices, market share, or technical bravado. We must commit to **fairness**: inclusivity, transparency, proportionality, deliberation, and adaptability. We must design with the understanding that everyone matters, even those with less to vote, but more to lose.

The fair DAO will not be built in a day. But every vote, every proposal, every self-audit brings us closer. This is not the easy path. But it is the only one worthy of the decentralized future we claim to believe in.

Chapter 7: Tokenomics and the Ethics of Incentives

Summary

Every blockchain protocol is an economy in miniature. At the center of this economy is its token—a vessel of value, governance, access, and speculation. How tokens are designed, distributed, and rewarded is not just a technical decision; it is a statement of ethics.

Tokenomics is moral architecture.

In the hands of ethical builders, tokens empower participation, align incentives, and support regenerative communities. In the hands of opportunists, they become tools for extraction, manipulation, and exploitation. This chapter examines the ethical responsibility of token design and how misaligned incentives undermine trust, while principled economics can build resilient, equitable ecosystems.

The Hidden Power of Incentive Design

Tokens shape behavior. Their supply, distribution, unlock schedules, burn mechanisms, and staking rewards all serve one function: **to guide the actions of participants**.

Examples:

- If early insiders hold 80% of the supply, decentralization is a myth.
- If yield rewards are unsustainable, the platform becomes a Ponzi.
- If governance rights are gated behind tokens earned through speculation, community input is distorted.

Tokenomics is not a value-neutral system. It is **a programmable philosophy**.

Ethical vs. Unethical Token Design

Unethical Tokenomics	Ethical Tokenomics
Obfuscated token supply or inflation	Transparent supply with public emission schedule
Insider unlocks ahead of retail investors.	Fair vesting with lockups for founders/advisors
Yield models dependent on new user deposits	Sustainable returns backed by real economic use
Hype-based launches (celebrity pumps, FOMO)	Gradual release with real utility and education
Governance concentrated in early backers.	Broad token holder participation rights

Ethics in tokenomics means accountability, balance, and restraint.

Ponzinomics: The Ethics of False Yield

Many protocols boast double-digit APYs—some even in the hundreds or thousands. But often, these returns are funded not by productive economic activity, but by:

- New investor capital (classic pyramid dynamics).
- Token inflation without real value creation.
- Hyper-leveraged staking derivatives.

This isn't sustainable finance. It's a yield theater.

Ethical tokenomics:

- Ties returns to **real-world asset performance**, usage, or service provision.
- Caps yields to protect platform longevity.
- Requires disclosures that explain where rewards come from, who pays, and how long they last.

Investors deserve truth, not engineered dopamine.

Airdrops, Gamification, and Behavioral Engineering

Tokens are also tools of influence. Airdrops, rewards, referral incentives, and staking boosts are all behavioral nudges. But ethical builders must ask:

- Are we rewarding learning—or speculation?
- Are we gamifying responsible engagement—or addicting users?
- Are referral bonuses transparent—or creating pyramid-like pressure?

There is nothing inherently wrong with incentives. But they must be:

- Disclosed fully.
- Modeled for long-term effects.
- Designed to **reward alignment, not manipulation.**

Tokenization in Real Estate: A Special Responsibility

Tokenized real estate carries unique ethical risks. The temptation to maximize token demand through inflated projections or artificial scarcity can:

- Mislead small investors.
- Disrupt tenant stability.
- Create volatility in essential housing.

Ethical property tokens:

- Reflect **actual cash flow** or underlying asset appreciation.
- Limit speculative flipping or fractional resale fees.
- Set clear rules for liquidation, maintenance, and reserve capital.

You are not just tokenizing capital. You are tokenizing **shelter, community, and long-term trust.**

Fair Launch and Distribution Ethics

Who gets the tokens—and when—is one of the most ethically loaded decisions in a project.

Guiding questions:

- Do early insiders have an unfair advantage?

- Was the community involved from day one?
- Are distribution mechanics (airdrops, presales, auctions) designed to promote **access or exclusivity**?

Tools for ethical distribution:

- **Retroactive rewards** for contributors and users.
- **Public sale tranches** with low per-wallet caps.
- **Community liquidity pools,** reserved for local stakeholders.

Access to upside should not be gated by capital alone.

Ethical Exit Strategies

Many projects fail, but how they fail matters.

Unethical exits:

- Silent rug pulls.
- Sudden unlocks and sell-offs.
- Transferring tokens to new chains without honoring old commitments.

Ethical exits include:

- On-chain treasury redistribution protocols.
- Optional buyouts or equity swaps for token holders.
- Transparent communication of failure timelines and funding statuses.

A failed protocol can still **leave a legacy of trust**—if it exits responsibly.

Conclusion: Designing for Regenerative Value

In DeFi and tokenized real estate, tokenomics is not just about price. It's about **purpose**. Ethical token design is the foundation for:

- Sustainable community growth.
- Resilient governance.
- Long-term investor trust.

Tokens can incentivize the best in human behavior—or the worst. The difference is design.

If we are building a new financial world, we must build it with care: one token, one stakeholder, and one incentive at a time.

Chapter 7: Expansion

I. Introduction: Every Token Is a Choice

Every blockchain project, at its core, is more than just a collection of code, interfaces, or digital signatures. It is an economy in miniature, complete with currency, incentives, and a set of programmable rules that guide who benefits, who participates, and who bears the risk. At the heart of these new economies lies the token, a vessel of value, governance, access, and, often, speculation.

The design of a token—its issuance, distribution, rewards, utility, and governance rights—is not a value-neutral technical act. It is a series of decisions, each carrying ethical consequences. The difference between a sustainable, inclusive protocol and a manipulative, extractive one is rarely found in the whitepaper's technical appendix. It is found in the moral logic of its tokenomics.

This chapter makes the case that **tokenomics is moral architecture**—an invisible, programmable structure—that can either build resilience, participation, and trust, or create new forms of exclusion, addiction, and abuse. It draws on industry experience, global perspectives, and first-person accounts to illuminate how the incentives we design will ultimately shape the kind of world blockchain delivers.

II. The Hidden Power of Incentive Design

Tokens are not mere "points" or "rewards," but programmable levers of human behavior. Their supply, initial distribution, unlock schedule, burn mechanisms, staking models, and reward systems guide the actions of every participant: users, developers, investors, and even outside observers.

Case Study: The Early-Insider Trap

Many DeFi projects launch with a fanfare of 'community ownership,' but early insiders, advisors, and backers quietly receive the lion's share of tokens before the public ever sees the interface.

Months later, as price rises, these insiders unlock and sell, triggering a cascade of panic as retail investors realize the myth of decentralization was just that—A myth.

Real-World Analogy: Central Bank Policy

In the traditional economy, central banks carefully manage interest rates, money supply, and incentives for lending or saving. A reckless or opaque central bank can trigger inflation, bubbles, and crashes. In blockchain, project founders and DAOs act as the "central bankers" of their own economies, wielding even greater power, often without external oversight or accountability.

First-Person Account:
"I joined a protocol because it promised fair staking rewards. But after the first year, most of the rewards went to addresses created before launch. The rest of us were just exit liquidity for insiders."
— Jasmine, DeFi user, Toronto

Tokenomics as Social Engineering

When engineered thoughtfully, incentives can:

- Encourage education, participation, and healthy governance.
- Fund real-world infrastructure, open-source development, or sustainable dividends.
- Align the long-term interests of users, builders, and capital providers.

When misaligned, incentives can:

- Drive unsustainable speculation, volatility, and addiction.
- Concentrate power and wealth in a handful of wallets.

- Create bubbles, Ponzi dynamics, and collapses that destroy trust.

III. Ethical vs. Unethical Token Design: Principles and Practices

A token is a promise, a declaration about the values and priorities of a protocol. The difference between ethical and unethical tokenomics is often hidden in the fine print, the vesting schedules, or the economics of yield.

Hallmarks of Unethical Tokenomics

- **Obfuscated supply and inflation:** Projects conceal true supply, hide mint functions, or issue new tokens without warning.
- **Insider unlocks:** Founders and advisors enjoy early liquidity while retail investors face lockups, dilution, or missed opportunities.
- **Ponzinomics:** Yields are paid out not from real economic activity, but from new deposits, resembling classic pyramid schemes.
- **Hype and FOMO-based launches:** Tokens are pushed with celebrity endorsements, engineered scarcity, and 'limited-time' offers, preying on fear of missing out.
- **Governance centralization:** Voting rights or protocol changes are reserved for early backers, undermining the premise of community-driven development.

Hallmarks of Ethical Tokenomics

- **Transparent supply and emission:** All tokenomics—supply, minting, burns, emissions—are public, auditable, and fixed in advance or subject to transparent DAO control.
- **Fair vesting and lockups:** Founders, advisors, and insiders face long lockups or slow release, with no privileged exit paths over retail participants.
- **Sustainable yields:** Returns are funded by real usage—transaction fees, lending revenue, or asset appreciation—not by unsustainable inflation or new deposits.
- **Gradual, utility-based launches:** Token release is tied to real use-cases, product milestones, and community learning, not just

speculation.
- **Broad, accessible governance:** All token holders (or even non-holders) can propose and vote, with systems in place to avoid plutocracy.

Industry Example:
A leading decentralized storage protocol implemented a five-year linear vesting for founders and investors, required a public audit of all emission schedules, and capped governance power to prevent any entity from exceeding 10% of total voting rights.

IV. Ponzinomics: The Lure and Lie of False Yield

Nowhere is the ethical risk of tokenomics more acute than in the proliferation of high-yield, "APY-as-a-service" protocols. Some promise double-, triple-, even quadruple-digit annual returns, dwarfing anything available in traditional finance. Yet beneath the surface, many of these yields are illusory, funded not by productive economic activity but by a musical chairs of new deposits.

Anatomy of a Yield Trap

- New users deposit tokens to receive eye-popping APYs.
- Early participants receive outsized rewards, fueling social media buzz and FOMO.
- As the protocol grows, the token price becomes increasingly dependent on a constant influx of new capital.
- When growth stalls or a large holder exits, rewards collapse, price plunges, and late entrants are left holding the bag.

The Social Cost

For every early winner, dozens (or thousands) lose, sometimes their entire savings. A false sense of community is fostered through memes and viral marketing, even as the system's collapse is inevitable by design.

First-Person Account:
"I was lured by a 400% APY on a staking platform. For months, it worked—until one day the rewards dried up and the price tanked. I

realized the only real source of yield was the next guy in line. It was a casino with a blockchain logo."
— Mikkel, Retail Investor, Copenhagen

The Ethical Response

Ethical projects:

- Tie rewards to real usage: Storage provided, loans originated, transactions processed, or property rented.
- Cap yields at sustainable levels, disclosing risk and time horizons.
- Require protocols to explain, in simple terms, where yields come from, who pays, and how long they can last.

V. Airdrops, Gamification, and the Psychology of Engagement

Tokens are also tools of influence used to reward, nudge, and sometimes manipulate user behavior. Airdrops, referral incentives, staking boosts, and points programs can be harnessed to build vibrant communities or to addict users to ever-higher risk and volatility.

Airdrops: Gifts or Traps?

Airdrops are often framed as 'democratizing' token distribution. But they can become cynical marketing, with sybil attacks (fake user farming), insider allocations, or sudden dumps that destroy token value.

Gamification: Engagement or Addiction?

Leaderboards, yield quests, and badge systems can incentivize learning and participation. But when designed without ethical guardrails, they create a dopamine loop, encouraging compulsive trading, reckless staking, and financial loss.

First-Person Perspective:
"At first, I loved completing quests for token rewards. But it soon felt like a slot machine—each badge made me want to risk more, even when I didn't understand the product."
— Sasha, User, Ukraine

Referral Systems: Growth vs. Pyramid Pressure

Referral bonuses can help protocols scale and reward early adopters. But when structured with exponential rewards, they resemble pyramid schemes, encouraging users to shill tokens for personal gain, regardless of real utility.

Ethical Guidelines

- Disclose all incentives, risks, and odds of reward, clearly and accessibly.
- Model and test long-term effects before launch; run pilots with opt-out and feedback channels.
- Reward behaviors that align with protocol health: education, governance, responsible use—not just trading or speculation.

VI. Tokenization in Real Estate: Unique Responsibilities

Tokenizing real estate adds a layer of complexity and ethical risk, which is not present in digital-only protocols. Property is shelter, community, and intergenerational wealth. Its volatility or misuse can destroy lives, not just portfolios.

Dangers of Speculative Property Tokens

- Inflated projections and artificial scarcity can mislead small investors.
- Over-gamified token markets can create volatility that spills into rent, tenancy, and local economies.
- Liquidity and flipping incentives may encourage absentee ownership, gentrification, or even "eviction by DAO."

Industry Example:
A U.S. property tokenization platform collapsed after global speculators outbid local residents, then voted to raise rents and flip properties rapidly. Displaced tenants organized a boycott and lawsuit, prompting regulatory intervention and industry-wide scrutiny.

Ethical Property Tokenomics

- Token returns should reflect actual cash flows—rent received,

property appreciation—rather than speculative trading volume.
- Speculative flipping is discouraged through minimum hold periods, high exit fees, or local resident buy-in rights.
- Protocols require full disclosure of maintenance reserves, liquidation rules, and tenant protections.
- Community and nonprofit set-asides ensure local voices and long-term stewardship.

First-Person Account:
"We bought tokens in a building that promised to 'democratize real estate.' A year later, rents were doubled, and we were priced out. The DAO members were anonymous and unreachable. It was digital gentrification."
— Martina, Former Tenant, Spain

VII. Fair Launch and Distribution Ethics

Perhaps no decision is more ethically charged than who gets the tokens, when, and at what price. Early access, insider rounds, airdrops, public sales, and liquidity mining all carry their own risks and opportunities for abuse or unfairness.

The Early Mover Advantage

Insider and venture rounds have a legitimate place—funding development and scaling—but must be balanced with vesting schedules, transparent allocations, and community involvement from the start.

Community Involvement

Ethical launches actively involve their communities:

- **Retroactive rewards:** Contributors and early users receive tokens for work, not just speculation.
- **Public sale tranches:** Caps and lottery systems prevent whales from dominating supply.
- **Liquidity pools for locals:** In property or physical asset tokens, local stakeholders have reserved allocations at favorable terms.

Industry Spotlight:
A Southeast Asian DeFi project allowed only verified community members to participate in its first sale, using quadratic caps and anti-bot measures. The token reached a broad, diverse base, and the price was more stable post-launch.

Distribution and Long-Term Alignment

Ethical distribution mechanics align upside with contribution, not just capital. Protocols disclose all allocations, release schedules, and vesting conditions publicly, building trust before, during, and after launch.

VIII. Ethical Exit Strategies

Most protocols, even with the best intentions, will eventually fail, fork, or wind down. The ethics of exit are as important as the ethics of launch.

Unethical Exits

- Silent rug pulls, where founders disappear with user funds.
- Sudden unlocks, mass sell-offs, or dumping of treasury assets to cover debts.
- Migrating to new chains or versions without honoring legacy token commitments.

Ethical Exits

- **On-chain treasury redistribution:** Unspent funds are returned to users or donated to public goods and ecosystem development.
- **Buyout or swap offers:** Token holders receive fair value in new versions, forks, or mergers.
- **Transparent wind-downs:** Timelines, fund status, and options are communicated early, with support for affected users.

First-Person Account:
"The protocol I used failed, but the team explained everything—funds, next steps, who to contact. They even offered a partial buyback. I lost some money, but I gained trust in ethical builders."
— Diego, User, Argentina

IX. Tokenomics in a Global and Historical Context

Token design does not exist in a vacuum. Each country, region, and cultural context brings its own challenges and expectations.

Global Perspective

- **Africa:** Mobile-first DeFi projects are tying rewards to education modules, local remittance, and community lending circles, building resilience instead of just speculation.
- **Europe:** Stringent regulation and consumer protection laws incentivize projects to design for clarity, fairness, and sustainability.
- **Asia:** Gamification and community-based staking drive engagement, but platforms are experimenting with caps and minimum hold times to combat hyper-volatility.
- **Latin America:** Property tokenization projects have learned from crises, embedding social impact, local equity, and tenant protections in their tokenomics to avoid displacement.

Historical Lessons: Bubbles, Crashes, and Trust

- **Tulip Mania, South Sea Bubble, Dot-Com Crash:** Each was driven by new technology, promises of democratized wealth, and incentives misaligned with reality. When the music stopped, trust was destroyed for years—in some cases, decades.
- **Modern Central Banking:** The hard-won lesson is that transparency, accountability, and restraint in incentives prevent crisis and build long-term prosperity.

X. Designing for Regenerative Value

The future of DeFi and tokenized assets will be written by those who understand that **tokenomics is not just about price; it's about purpose**.

Tokens can be a force for good, aligning stakeholders, funding innovation, and building resilient, equitable systems. Or they can enable the worst forms of extraction, manipulation, and ruin.

What Regenerative Tokenomics Looks Like

- Sustainable returns tied to real-world use.
- Incentives for participation, learning, and governance—not just trading.
- Mechanisms to prevent plutocracy, addiction, and exclusion.
- Transparency and fairness in both launch and exit.
- A commitment to ongoing audit, iteration, and user empowerment.

First-Person Vision:
"If we get tokenomics right, we can build economies that heal, not just grow. Where upside is shared, risk is managed, and communities last longer than any hype cycle."
— Ayodele, Protocol Designer, Nigeria

XI. Conclusion: One Token, One Stakeholder, One World

The ethics of tokenomics is not an academic exercise; it is the foundation of a new financial world. Every design choice shapes who participates, who wins, and who is left out. The incentives we encode today will echo for decades, building or eroding trust, resilience, and opportunity.

As founders, investors, regulators, and community members, the challenge is to ask:

- Who benefits from this token, and how?
- Is the incentive sustainable, just, and honest?
- Does the protocol empower its users or exploit them?
- Will its failure leave ruin or a legacy of trust?

Tokens can incentivize the best in human nature—or the worst. The difference is in design. As we build the next era of finance and ownership, let us do so with care, humility, and a fierce commitment to ethical purpose.

Tokenomics is not just economics. It is ethics, codified.

Chapter 8: Privacy, Surveillance, and Digital Identity

Summary

Blockchain was born in the shadow of mistrust—of central banks, opaque institutions, and digital surveillance. It promised a world where trust could be minimized, privacy preserved, and autonomy protected. Yet as decentralized systems scale, a paradox emerges:

Transparency is absolute, but privacy is vanishing.

Every transaction, every vote, every token swap is visible to anyone, forever. What was once hailed as an immutable audit trail is now—without ethical safeguards—a potential tool of mass surveillance, coercion, and exclusion.

In this chapter, we explore the ethical balance between **transparency and privacy**, and the urgent need for identity systems that empower users without exposing them.

The Myth of Anonymity

Early blockchain advocates believed anonymity was native to the technology. In reality, most blockchains are **pseudonymous—not anonymous**—and increasingly de-anonymized by:

- On-chain analytics firms.
- Wallet clustering and metadata scraping.
- Wallet blacklisting and geolocation surveillance.

Your wallet tells a story: what you earn, where you live, who you engage with, and when. In the wrong hands, this becomes **a surveillance engine**.

Ethical platforms must design systems that preserve **user agency over visibility.**

The Right to Privacy Is a Human Right

Privacy is not about hiding. It's about choosing what to share, when, and with whom.

- Financial privacy protects vulnerable users from exploitation.
- Identity privacy prevents targeting based on race, gender, or location.
- Data privacy ensures that your transaction history isn't used against you by employers, governments, or malicious actors.

Ethical blockchain design respects privacy as a **core human dignity**, not a fringe concern.

Programmable Privacy: The Path Forward

Rather than seeing privacy and compliance as opposites, ethical builders can engineer systems that offer:

- **Selective disclosure** – Reveal only what's required to a counterparty or regulator.
- **Zero-knowledge proofs (ZKPs)** – Prove identity, age, or asset control without exposing the data.
- **Data expiration** – Automatically sunset sensitive data unless renewed by consent.
- **Opt-in audit trails** – Let users activate transparency when legally required.

These tools give users control without compromising legal accountability.

On-Chain Reputation: Promise and Peril

As DeFi expands, protocols are increasingly turning to on-chain behavior for:

- Credit scoring.
- Borrow limits.
- Access tiers.

This creates **reputation systems** built on immutable histories.

But if not designed ethically, these systems:

- Penalize users forever for past mistakes.
- Reinforce wealth-based privilege.

- Create identity lock-ins with no appeal or redress.

To build a fair, on-chain reputation:

- Include **grace periods**, privacy resets, and appeals.
- Use **context-aware scoring**, not binary yes/no flags.
- Allow **portable reputation** across chains and ecosystems.

People are not their past. Code should reflect that.

Ethical KYC/AML: Beyond the Database

Compliance with anti-money laundering laws is essential, but the '**how**' matters deeply.

Unethical KYC:

- Collects sensitive documents, then sells or misuses them.
- Centralizes identity data in breach-prone silos.
- Refuses service without appeal or explanation.

Ethical KYC:

- Uses **verifiable credentials** that stay with the user.
- Leverages **decentralized identifiers (DIDs)**.
- Integrates with **privacy-preserving identity wallets**.
- Enables **jurisdiction-specific disclosure**—only when required.

Identity can be verified without being exploited.

Tokenized Real Estate: Privacy in Physical Space

Property is not just digital—it's lived in, walked through, and deeply personal. In tokenized housing:

- Should tenants know who holds the tokens on their home?
- Should token holders see tenant payment data?
- What happens if ownership data leaks or is targeted?

Ethical platforms must:

- Separate investment data from tenant data.
- Use legal entities or blind trusts for ownership if needed.

- Implement **privacy firewalls** between the occupant and investor.

Homes are not for surveillance; they are for safety.

Global Privacy Regulations: Aligning with Law

Privacy ethics also align with growing legal mandates:

- **GDPR (EU):** Data minimization, consent, and right to be forgotten.
- **CCPA (California):** Opt-outs, data portability, and breach notifications.
- **OECD Guidelines:** Fairness, transparency, and accountability in data processing.

Blockchains may be immutable, but **privacy rights must be adaptable.** Ethical platforms use technical workarounds (e.g., off-chain storage, ZKPs) to ensure compliance with the spirit and letter of the law.

Conclusion: Transparency with Consent, Privacy by Design

Ethical blockchain systems embrace **both transparency and privacy** but with nuance, context, and user choice. Surveillance capitalism must not be rebranded as "Web3 analytics." Privacy is not a bug in decentralization. It is a **moral and strategic imperative**.

We must build systems where users do not fear exposure, manipulation, or punishment for simply participating. Where identity is secure, voluntary, and portable.

Because a truly decentralized world is not one where everything is visible—it's one where **everyone is safe.**

Chapter 8: Expansion

I. Introduction: The Paradox at the Heart of Blockchain

When Satoshi Nakamoto released the Bitcoin whitepaper in 2008, privacy was not merely an afterthought; it was a principle. The entire architecture of blockchain was designed in response to growing mistrust of centralized banks, opaque financial intermediaries, and the digital surveillance quietly creeping across the global internet. The earliest crypto communities believed they had found the perfect alchemy: A system where trust was minimized, power decentralized, and privacy preserved by design.

But as blockchain has scaled from hobbyist experiment to the backbone of new economies—powering everything from DeFi to tokenized real estate—a paradox has emerged.

On one hand, blockchains are lauded for their radical transparency: every transaction, vote, and smart contract execution is auditable by anyone, anywhere, forever. On the other hand, this 'glass ledger' can become a tool for mass surveillance, coercion, discrimination, and exclusion, if not balanced by deliberate, ethical safeguards.

Privacy, far from being solved by the advent of blockchain, is now the site of a new and urgent battle. The choices made by today's builders, regulators, and investors will determine whether decentralized systems liberate individuals from surveillance—or simply automate new forms of exposure and control.

II. The Myth of Anonymity: Blockchain's Public Ledger and Its Limits

In the popular imagination, blockchain is synonymous with anonymity. Early news stories painted Bitcoin and its peers as havens for the untraceable and the underground. Reality is both more complex and, for most users, far less private.

Pseudonymity, Not Anonymity

Most blockchains are pseudonymous; users interact with the network through cryptographic addresses, not legal names. At first glance, this appears anonymous, but the ledger is permanent, public, and richly detailed.

As blockchain analytics firms have shown, these digital footprints are easily de-anonymized:

- Wallet clustering links addresses to real-world identities through transaction patterns.
- Metadata scraping reveals geolocations, device fingerprints, and behavioral signatures.

- On-chain analytics track fund flows, identify sources and sinks, and flag "suspicious" activity for law enforcement or private actors.
- Blacklisting wallets is now routine, triggered by regulatory mandates or even private disputes.

First-Person Account:
"I thought my crypto wallet was anonymous. But after I bought tokens from an exchange, suddenly my transactions were flagged on social media. Friends traced every move—what I bought, when I staked, even how much I sent to my partner. It was like my bank account was public, except everyone could see it."
— Carlos, Retail User, Spain

Surveillance in the Age of Web3

Blockchain's radical transparency, unmitigated, can be weaponized. Employers, governments, insurance companies, and malicious actors can mine the ledger to reveal financial habits, political affiliations, geographic movements, and social networks. In some regimes, activists and journalists have been targeted through their transaction histories. In open marketplaces, "whale watching" exposes high-net-worth individuals to phishing, scams, or even physical harm.

The lesson: Anonymity is a myth. Privacy is not the default state of decentralized systems, but a design choice that must be intentionally engineered.

III. The Right to Privacy is a Human Right

The right to privacy is enshrined in the Universal Declaration of Human Rights, the International Covenant on Civil and Political Rights, and countless national constitutions. It is not merely the right to hide, but the right to choose what to share, when, and with whom.

The Social and Economic Value of Privacy

Privacy is more than an individual preference. It is the foundation of dignity, autonomy, and safe participation in society. In the digital economy, privacy protects:

- **Vulnerable users** from exploitation, such as political dissidents, minorities, or survivors of abuse.
- **Financial security**, preventing targeting by thieves, extortionists, or unfair discrimination by insurers and employers.
- **Identity sovereignty**, ensuring people are not permanently branded by past mistakes, circumstances, or rumors.

Industry Example:
In certain countries, LGBTQ+ individuals have used cryptocurrencies to escape surveillance and financial exclusion. But the same transparency that enables accountability can also expose users to blackmail or state harassment if not carefully protected.

Privacy as a Design Principle

Ethical blockchain design treats privacy as a core human dignity. The aim is not to eliminate transparency, but to give users agency—control over their own data, histories, and reputations.

IV. Programmable Privacy: The Path Forward

Too often, privacy and compliance are seen as opposites: privacy for the anarchists, compliance for the grownups. This is a false binary. Ethical and future-ready blockchain systems can use advanced cryptography and selective disclosure to empower users, without undermining regulatory needs or the integrity of markets.

Selective Disclosure

Instead of an all-or-nothing ledger, platforms can let users reveal only what is needed—age, residency, or proof of funds—while withholding all other personal data. Only counterparties or auditors with a legitimate interest see the relevant details.

Zero-Knowledge Proofs (ZKPs)

ZKPs allow a user to prove a fact (e.g., "I am over 18," "I control 100 tokens," "My funds are not from a blacklist") without revealing the underlying data. As the technology matures, ZKPs can power KYC, voting, and credit systems that respect both privacy and compliance.

Industry Case:
A European DeFi lending protocol uses ZKPs to prove loan eligibility: Borrowers demonstrate sufficient collateral and non-sanctioned status without exposing their full wallets or identities. Lenders see only what they need to assess risk.

Data Expiration and User Consent

Blockchain data is by default permanent. But new tools allow for "data expiration," letting users set information to sunset after a period, unless they renew consent. This prevents the buildup of permanent and all-revealing records.

Opt-In Audit Trails

Users can enable transparency for legal or tax reasons, generating cryptographically signed audit logs only when required by courts, regulators, or contracts. Outside those circumstances, their activity remains private by default.

First-Person Account

"I'm a journalist in a country with strict controls. Using ZKPs, I can prove I've paid for services or accessed my salary without showing the world every move I make. It's the first time I've felt safe online in years."
— Noor, Journalist, Middle East

V. On-Chain Reputation: Promise and Peril

One of the most powerful—and dangerous—innovations in Web3 is the rise of on-chain reputation. Protocols increasingly turn to blockchain data to determine:

- Credit scores for DeFi lending.
- Borrowing or trading limits.
- Access tiers, privileges, and even voting power.

The Perils of Immutable Histories

If not designed with care, these systems can:

- Penalize users forever for past mistakes or circumstances, even if they change.
- Reinforce wealth-based privilege, rewarding those with early capital or advantageous networks.
- Create identity lock-ins, where a lost wallet or false flag brands a user with no path to appeal or redemption.

Case Study:
A prominent NFT platform denied access to an artist based on a single flagged transaction, even after the user proved the issue was an honest error. With no appeals process, the artist's career was effectively blocked.

Designing Fair On-Chain Reputation

Ethical reputation systems must:

- Include grace periods, privacy resets, and a clear appeals process.
- Use context-aware scoring, weighting recent and positive behavior.
- Allow users to port reputation across chains, wallets, and ecosystems—so one misstep or compromised key does not doom a digital future.

Industry Spotlight:
A decentralized identity project in Latin America allows users to "reset" their reputation by completing community service, education, or dispute resolution steps, recognizing that people are more than their past.

VI. Ethical KYC/AML: Beyond the Database

Anti-money laundering (AML) and Know Your Customer (KYC) checks are now table stakes for blockchain projects that touch real assets, fiat on-ramps, or regulated markets. But the *how* of compliance matters as much as the *what*.

The Unethical Model

- Sensitive documents are collected—passports, driver's licenses, utility bills—then stored in breach-prone central databases.
- Data is resold to advertisers, marketers, or worse, data brokers.

- Access is denied without a clear reason, explanation, or appeal.

The Ethical Model

- **Verifiable credentials:** Users control their own KYC data, issuing cryptographic proofs when needed, without sharing raw documents.
- **Decentralized identifiers (DIDs):** Identity is anchored to the user, not a platform—portable, revocable, and updatable.
- **Privacy-preserving wallets:** Data is stored locally or encrypted on the blockchain, not in centralized silos.
- **Jurisdiction-specific disclosure:** Only the data required by law is shared, only with authorized parties, and only with user consent.

Industry Example:
A Singapore-based exchange partners with an identity wallet provider. Users complete KYC once, then control what information is shared for each transaction, retaining audit logs and instant opt-out at any time.

First-Person Perspective

"After a major exchange hack, I worried my passport was for sale on the dark web. Now I use a self-sovereign ID wallet—no more uploading the same document everywhere. I choose what to share and when."
— Malik, Entrepreneur, UAE

VII. Tokenized Real Estate: Privacy in Physical Space

Tokenization brings privacy risks beyond the digital ledger. When property—homes, apartments, offices—is fractionalized and sold as tokens, new ethical dilemmas emerge.

Who Sees What?

- Should tenants know which wallets own tokens in their home or building? What if owners are anonymous DAOs or international funds?
- Should token holders see tenant payment or occupancy data? What happens if this data is leaked, manipulated, or sold?
- If ownership data is public, tenants can be targeted, tracked, or

harassed by activists, criminals, or even unscrupulous landlords.

Industry Case:

A U.S. property DAO posted rental payment histories on-chain for "transparency." When data was scraped and used by insurance companies to deny claims or raise premiums, tenants revolted, and the platform faced regulatory sanctions.

Ethical Best Practices

- **Separate investment from tenant data:** Use legal entities or blind trusts to mask ownership where necessary, especially in sensitive regions.
- **Privacy firewalls:** Only aggregate, anonymized data is shared with token holders. Individual payment or occupancy data is kept off-chain or encrypted.
- **Consent and opt-out:** Tenants must be informed of what data is collected and can veto non-essential disclosures.

First-Person Account:
"We found out our rent data was posted online, and suddenly, our insurance and job applications became harder. We were promised decentralization, but got surveillance instead."
— Lana, Tenant, New York

VIII. Global Privacy Regulations: Aligning with Law

The ethical imperative for privacy is increasingly backed by legal mandates, especially in the world's largest economies.

GDPR (European Union)

- **Data minimization:** Only the data strictly necessary for the service is collected.
- **Consent:** Users must actively agree to data processing and can withdraw consent at any time.
- **Right to be forgotten:** Users can demand erasure of their data.
- **Portability:** Data must be accessible and transferable on user request.

CCPA (California)

- **Opt-outs:** Users can refuse the sale or sharing of data.
- **Transparency:** Users have a right to know what data is collected and how it's used.
- **Breach notifications:** Companies must inform users of any unauthorized access or data loss.

OECD Guidelines

- **Fairness, transparency, and accountability** in all data processing, with a bias toward user protection.

Blockchain's Dilemma

Blockchains, by nature, are immutable. But privacy rights must be adaptable. Solutions include:

- Storing sensitive data off-chain, with only pointers or proofs on the blockchain.
- Using ZKPs for on-chain attestations that do not reveal underlying data.
- Building "right to be forgotten" tools at the wallet or dApp layer, deleting local data, and revoking on-chain access.

Industry Spotlight:
A major European NFT platform developed a two-tier storage system: art and sensitive metadata are off-chain, user actions on-chain are limited to public keys, and GDPR compliance is audited annually.

IX. Privacy, Surveillance, and Digital Identity in a Global Context

Asia: Pushing for Privacy Amid State Surveillance

In China and some Southeast Asian nations, blockchain has been both a tool for individual empowerment and a new vector for state control. Projects that wish to operate safely for users must build opt-in privacy at every level—and be transparent about risks.

Africa: Mobile-First Identity and Consent

In Nigeria and Kenya, mobile identity wallets are empowering unbanked populations to access services, credit, and voting, often with privacy-by-default. Success hinges on clear user education and granular control over consent.

Latin America: Fighting Corruption and Surveillance

Argentinian and Mexican civic tech startups are building privacy-preserving ledgers for property and voting—balancing transparency for anti-corruption with the need to protect activists, journalists, and everyday users.

Europe: The Privacy Gold Standard

European dApps and exchanges are under pressure to implement GDPR not just as law, but as a market differentiator. Platforms that fail to comply face exclusion from the world's largest digital market.

North America: From Silicon Valley to Surveillance Valley

The U.S. is home to both privacy pioneers and surveillance giants. The lesson for blockchain projects: user choice, clear terms, and opt-out must be standard—not just marketing.

X. Industry Case Studies and Failures

Failure: De-Anonymization and "Web3 Doxxing"

A high-profile NFT collector was targeted and extorted after on-chain data revealed their physical address. The information had been pieced together from transaction patterns, ENS domains, and social media.

Success: Privacy-First DeFi Lending

A Swiss lending protocol built on ZKPs grew rapidly by assuring borrowers and lenders that no sensitive data would ever be shared—unless required by a legal warrant, then only to the specific party. Transparency for trust, privacy for safety.

XI. Designing for Privacy—Frameworks and Tools

a) **Minimum-necessary data:** Always ask, "What is the least information needed to provide this service or compliance?"
b) **Privacy-by-default settings:** Users opt in to public or third-party access, never the reverse.
c) **Audit and review:** Annual or ongoing privacy audits by independent experts, published for user scrutiny.
d) **Portable, self-sovereign identities:** Give users one ID for all Web3, owned by them—not the platform.
e) **Contextual reputation and scoring:** No single flag or score can define a user's rights. All scoring is time-bound, explainable, and appealable.

XII. The Strategic and Moral Imperative

Privacy is not a 'bug' in decentralization, nor an afterthought. It is both a strategic necessity—protecting users from harm, regulation, and exclusion—and a moral imperative, upholding dignity in a digital world.

First-Person Reflection:
"Privacy gives me freedom—not to hide, but to live, create, and participate without fear. That is what drew me to blockchain. We must protect it as fiercely as any other right."
— Isabel, Artist and DAO Contributor, Brazil

XIII. Conclusion: Transparency with Consent, Privacy by Design

The future of blockchain—whether it liberates or surveils, includes or excludes—will be decided by the design choices made today. We must build systems where users do not fear exposure, manipulation, or punishment for simply participating, where identity is secure, voluntary, and portable, where transparency serves the public good, and privacy guards the individual.

Because a truly decentralized world is not one where everything is visible; it's one where everyone is safe.

Chapter 9: Failure, Exit, and Ethical Wind-downs

All systems fail. The ethical test is not whether we can avoid collapse, but **how we respond to it**. In blockchain—where platforms are global, money is programmable, and code is immutable—the failure of a project doesn't just result in lost capital. It can mean:

- Investor devastation,
- Loss of housing or yield,
- Broken governance mechanisms,
- And reputational fallout that taints the broader ecosystem.

Unlike traditional businesses that file for bankruptcy under formal processes, decentralized projects often fade without accountability. This absence of structured failure planning poses a deep ethical challenge.

Failure must be designed ethically, transparently, and with safeguards.

Why Failure Matters in a Decentralized World

Traditional finance has built-in safety nets: deposit insurance, bankruptcy courts, and regulatory oversight. In contrast, DeFi and tokenized systems often operate in a vacuum of:

- Legal frameworks,
- Investor guarantees,
- Operational continuity planning.

This leaves stakeholders—especially non-technical ones—vulnerable to total loss. Worse, it erodes public trust in innovation. A few catastrophic failures can set back entire industries.

Ethical platforms must plan for worst-case scenarios with the same rigor they plan for scale.

The Anatomy of Ethical Wind-Downs

An ethical wind-down process must include:

1. **Transparency**
    - Public notice of insolvency, code failure, or governance breakdown.
    - Timeline of expected service reductions or shutdowns.
    - Full disclosure of remaining treasury, assets, and liabilities.
2. **Orderly Asset Distribution**
    - Predefined payout logic embedded in smart contracts.
    - Treasury prioritization (e.g., user funds before team payouts).
    - Community vote on asset reallocation (where feasible).
3. **Data Preservation and Export**
    - Export tools for user transaction history, staking records, and tax documentation.
    - Secure off-chain backups of governance logs or proposal archives.
4. **Legal and Regulatory Filings**
    - If under a DAO wrapper (e.g., Wyoming DAO LLC), initiate proper dissolution.
    - Notify token holders of final filings, K-1s, or capital loss documentation.
5. **Exit Communication and Support**
    - FAQs, help desk, and post-shutdown contact channels.
    - Guidance for claiming residual funds or migrating to successor protocols.

A failure does not have to be a betrayal if it is handled with transparency, fairness, and human care.

What Not to Do: The Ethics of Abandonment

The crypto space has seen numerous unethical exits:

- **Silent rug pulls** with no notice or refund.
- **Social media blackouts** as liquidity dries up.
- **Discord deletions**, shutting out user communities.
- **Token dumps** by insiders days before the collapse.

Each of these actions deepens harm and stains the integrity of Web3. Founders may think they're "cutting losses," but in reality, they're burning bridges across the industry.

The moral standard is simple: exit as honorably as you entered.

Pre-Built Wind-Down Mechanisms: A New Standard

Smart contracts and governance tools should include **pre-coded fail-safes** for dissolution, including:

- A minimum reserve held for user reimbursements.
- Automated treasury unwinding tied to DAO vote thresholds.
- "Graceful sunset" protocols for token deactivation.
- Multisig-triggered emergency pause or fund-lock options.

These mechanisms reduce emotional bias, last-minute chaos, and legal ambiguity.

Tokenized Real Estate: Ethical Risk Planning

When real-world assets are tokenized, failure can impact tenants, neighborhoods, and physical infrastructure.

Ethical real estate tokenization includes:

- Property-holding legal entities with continuity plans.
- Escrow reserves for taxes, maintenance, and repairs—even during platform closure.
- Governance clauses requiring a community vote before liquidating physical assets.
- Contractual safeguards to prevent displacement or foreclosure without due process.

When shelter is involved, failure ethics take on life-altering weight.

Reputation Is a Scarce Asset

Builders must recognize: how you fail is how you will be remembered.

Reputation in Web3 is both:

- Portable (via wallet history, GitHub contributions, proposal authorship), and
- Fragile (tied to narrative, perception, and digital trust).

A graceful shutdown can build founder credibility. It can attract support for future ventures. It can become part of a brand of **conscientious innovation**, not reckless speculation.

Conclusion: Designing for the End, Not Just the Start

Innovation without exit planning is irresponsible. Code that can deploy must also be able to **unwind**. Platforms that raise capital must also design for their ethical return.

This chapter is a call for maturity. For foresight. For a new standard in blockchain: where every launch includes a **final chapter already written**—not because we expect failure, but because we respect everyone involved if it happens.

The true measure of a project is not how it performs at its peak, but how it behaves when it ends.

Chapter 9: Expansion

I. Introduction: The Final Test of Innovation

All systems fail—eventually.

In both technology and finance, the true ethical test is not whether collapse can be avoided forever, but how leadership responds when collapse arrives. For centralized institutions, centuries of bankruptcy law, insurance, and regulatory intervention have established guardrails for orderly wind-down. In the world of blockchain, DeFi, and tokenized assets, however, the frontier mentality persists: innovation is fast, risk is high, and exit planning is often ignored—until disaster strikes.

Yet the reality is unavoidable. In decentralized finance, global tokenized real estate, and DAOs, the failure of a protocol can mean more than just a lost investment. It can lead to widespread financial devastation, the displacement of families, the breakdown of governance, and reputational harm that echoes across the entire ecosystem. Unlike a failed startup that quietly files bankruptcy and notifies its creditors, decentralized projects can dissolve into digital silence, leaving users, investors, tenants, and communities with nothing but confusion, loss, and distrust.

This chapter argues for a new, ethical standard: **Failure must be designed for**—transparently, rigorously, and with safeguards equal to those built for scale and success. The way a project exits is as consequential as the way it grows. In blockchain, **exit is ethics**.

II. Why Failure Matters in a Decentralized World

The myth of the unstoppable protocol, always "up only," is seductive. But history—and market cycles—reveal a harder truth: Even the most brilliant projects are subject to disruption, regulatory change, competition, technological obsolescence, or plain bad luck. When they fail, the consequences can be catastrophic for the most vulnerable stakeholders.

The Missing Safety Net

Traditional finance has spent centuries building resilience for failure:

- **Deposit insurance** shields savers in the event of bank insolvency.
- **Bankruptcy courts** orchestrate the fair division of assets, enabling reorganization or managed liquidation.
- **Regulatory oversight** enforces risk management, minimum reserves, and mandatory disclosures, so collapse is rarely a total surprise.

DeFi and tokenized systems, by contrast, often operate without:

- Legal frameworks for asset protection or transfer.
- Guarantees for investors, tenants, or users.
- Operational continuity or crisis planning.

This absence leaves stakeholders—especially non-technical users, renters, and small investors—vulnerable to total loss and abandonment.

Case Study: The DAO Hack and Community Fork

In 2016, the original DAO on Ethereum collapsed after a vulnerability was exploited. Rather than an orderly wind-down, the event triggered a contentious hard fork, splitting the chain, community, and developer base. For many, the collapse was a clarion call: Without formalized processes for failure, the only remedy is chaos.

First-Person Account

"I invested in a yield protocol that went dark overnight. The Discord was deleted, the website vanished, and the tokens became worthless. I tried reaching out, but got no response. I didn't just lose money—I lost faith in the entire space."
— Malik, DeFi User, Malaysia

III. The Anatomy of Ethical Wind-Downs

To prevent such outcomes, ethical wind-down processes must be built into the DNA of every serious project. A graceful exit can protect users, honor the community, and preserve industry trust, even in the face of technical or financial failure.

Transparency: The First Duty

The moment a protocol recognizes imminent insolvency, code failure, or governance breakdown, **public notice** must be issued. This means:

- Announcing the nature of the problem, the timeline for service reduction or shutdown, and the expected impact.
- Publishing a full disclosure of treasury assets, remaining obligations, liabilities, and payout order.
- Ensuring ongoing communication—through FAQs, help desks, or community channels—so users are not left in the dark.

Orderly Asset Distribution

Ethical wind-downs require **predefined payout logic**, ideally embedded in smart contracts. This means:

- User deposits and unpaid claims are prioritized over founder or team payouts.
- Asset reallocation is managed transparently, with community votes or independent oversight where feasible.
- All transactions are logged, timestamped, and auditable for future reference.

Data Preservation and Export

Even as a system is shutting down, users deserve the ability to **export their transaction histories, staking records,** and **tax documentation**. Protocols should provide secure backups—both on-chain and off-chain—of all governance logs, proposals, and critical communications.

Legal and Regulatory Filings

Where projects have legal wrappers—such as a Wyoming DAO LLC or Swiss GmbH—ethical wind-down includes:

- Initiating proper legal dissolution, filing final regulatory documents, and notifying all token holders of their rights and obligations.
- Providing capital loss documentation (e.g., K-1s) for tax or accounting purposes.

Exit Communication and Support

Long after shutdown, channels must remain open for users to claim residual funds, migrate to successor protocols, or seek support in case of disputes. Community forums, archived FAQs, and a documented process for inquiries are marks of respect, not cost.

IV. What Not to Do: The Ethics of Abandonment

History is replete with examples of unethical exits, each eroding public trust and intensifying regulatory scrutiny.

The Silent Rug Pull

Some projects vanish overnight: founders disappear, websites and social media go dark, and treasury funds are siphoned to anonymous wallets. Users are left with illiquid tokens and no recourse.

Blackouts and Discord Deletions

The deletion of user forums and Discords shuts out communities, erases collective memory, and signals a refusal to accept responsibility.

Insider Token Dumps

Team members or advisors dump their tokens on secondary markets in the days before collapse, triggering price crashes and transferring risk to unsuspecting users.

First-Person Account:
"The team that built our platform was everywhere during the bull market. The moment things turned, they ghosted us. The social contract was broken—not just the code."
— Larissa, NFT Collector, Brazil

The Aftermath

Every abandonment not only destroys the reputation of those involved but also stains the wider ecosystem. Regulators, journalists, and public critics seize on such examples to paint all blockchain projects as reckless or predatory.

V. Pre-Built Wind-Down Mechanisms: A New Standard

Ethical exit is not an afterthought. It must be **designed** and **coded in from the start**.

Smart Contract Fail-Safes

- **Minimum reserves**: Protocols can require a set percentage of treasury to be reserved for user reimbursement, only releasable through multi-sig or DAO vote in case of dissolution.
- **Automated unwinding**: Contracts can trigger emergency sunset protocols, distributing residual funds to users in proportion to their holdings.
- **Emergency pause and lock**: Multi-sig or governance-triggered

fund locks can prevent last-minute drain or manipulation.

- **DAO vote thresholds**: Sunset can be triggered by community consensus, not just founders or insiders.

Scenario Planning

Just as financial regulators demand "living wills" for big banks, major blockchain projects should publish scenario plans for wind-down: Who is responsible? How are funds accessed and distributed? What is the timeline for communication and support?

Industry Example:
A Swiss asset-backed token project published a full wind-down protocol on launch, including automated payout logic, tax document generation, and off-chain legal compliance. When regulatory pressure forced closure, users were reimbursed transparently, and the team's reputation survived.

VI. Tokenized Real Estate: The Special Burden of Physical Assets

When blockchain platforms tokenize physical assets—homes, apartments, offices—failure carries not just financial risk, but the potential for real-world harm.

Displacement and Community Harm

- **Tenants** may face eviction, loss of services, or unsafe living conditions if maintenance stops.
- **Neighborhoods** can be destabilized by sudden liquidation, abandoned properties, or absentee token holders.
- **Physical infrastructure** may deteriorate, leading to long-term damage and legal liabilities.

Ethical Risk Planning

Tokenized real estate platforms must:

- **Hold property through legal entities** with built-in continuity plans, ensuring that maintenance, taxes, and repairs continue even if the protocol shuts down.
- **Maintain escrow reserves** dedicated to property upkeep during

wind-down.

- **Require community votes or local stakeholder consultation** before liquidating or transferring physical assets.
- **Contractual safeguards** must protect tenants from sudden displacement or foreclosure.

First-Person Account:
"When our building's token platform failed, we were terrified we'd be thrown out. But the protocol had escrow for repairs, and a local trust took over management. We stayed, and eventually bought a share of the building ourselves."
— Jomo, Tenant and Community Organizer, Kenya

Global Perspective

In Germany, city governments are partnering with real estate DAOs to ensure that, in case of wind-down, assets revert to municipal trusts rather than speculators, preserving affordable housing and local stewardship.

VII. The Industry's Record: Lessons from Success and Failure

Case Study: The Unwind of a Major DeFi Protocol

A DeFi lending platform in North America collapsed after an oracle exploit drained reserves. Unlike most failures, the team immediately published full details, froze all operations, and opened daily community calls.

Smart contracts prioritized user withdrawal, leaving the team's own tokens unrecoverable. The core team posted public audits and FAQs, stayed active for months post-closure, and assisted users with tax and loss documentation.

The result: While investors still lost money, the team's reputation for transparency led to support for their next venture.

Case Study: The FTX Collapse and Its Fallout

When the FTX exchange imploded, the consequences were catastrophic: user deposits vanished, communications ceased, and a wave of lawsuits, investigations, and public anger followed. The absence of a transparent, pre-coded wind-down destroyed trust not just in FTX, but across centralized crypto finance.

Industry Success: The DAI Emergency Shutdown Protocol

MakerDAO, the issuer of DAI, has built an emergency shutdown into its core contracts. If triggered by a governance vote, all DAI can be redeemed for collateral, protecting holders from runaway risk.

While not perfect, it shows how protocols can embed wind-down into their architecture.

VIII. Data Preservation and Export: Respecting User Autonomy

Failure does not mean erasure. Ethical wind-downs ensure users retain access to their histories, balances, and rights:

- **Export tools** must enable users to download transaction records, staking logs, and governance votes for legal, tax, or migration purposes.
- **Open-sourcing code and archives** allows communities to fork or rebuild, continuing the project's mission even if leadership fails.
- **Secure off-chain backups** preserve knowledge for audit, academic research, or litigation.

Industry Example:
A failing NFT marketplace released its full codebase, database, and governance history under an open license, enabling former users to relaunch under new leadership.

IX. Legal and Regulatory Filings: Doing It by the Book

Ethical wind-downs require adherence to all legal obligations:

- **DAO wrappers** (e.g., Wyoming DAO LLCs) must be dissolved according to state law, with filings and notifications to all members.
- **Tax documents** (K-1s, capital loss statements) must be generated and distributed.

- **Final audits** and regulatory reports should be published, setting a precedent for future compliance and good faith.

First-Person Perspective:
"Our DeFi fund collapsed, but the legal entity filed every document. I claimed my loss on taxes and moved on, with closure and respect."
— Sophia, Investor, United States

X. Exit Communication and Support: Human Care Amid Collapse

Ethics demand more than just code. During and after wind-down, projects must provide **help desks, clear FAQs, live chat,** and **contact points**, even if only for a defined period. Abandonment is never ethical.

- Guidance for claiming residual funds
- Assistance with migration to new platforms
- Documenting "lessons learned" for future builders

Cultural Note

In Asian and African fintech, some platforms have adopted "exit ambassadors," dedicated staff whose sole job is to help users navigate failure, often earning the project long-term goodwill even after closure.

XI. The Moral and Reputational Asset: How You Fail is How You're Remembered

In blockchain, just like in life, **reputation is portable**. It follows founders across wallets, communities, and GitHub profiles. A graceful, transparent exit—one that minimizes harm, communicates openly, and respects users—can make all the difference for a team's next project, or even the broader ecosystem.

Historical Analogy: The Lehman Brothers Collapse

Thc 2008 collapse of Lehman Brothers was made worse by secretive, last-minute deals, misleading communication, and confusion. In contrast, the more transparent unwindings of Bear Stearns and Washington Mutual preserved some trust and mitigated contagion.

First-Person Account

"Our DAO failed, but the core devs stayed, helped us recover what we could, and owned their mistakes. I'll invest with them again—their word means something."
— Pieter, DAO Member, Netherlands

XII. Designing for the End: Wind-Down as the New Standard

Maturity in blockchain is not measured by price or hype, but by foresight, by the ability to anticipate failure and embed it in the design.

Framework for Ethical Wind-Downs

1. **Scenario Planning:** Identify triggers for exit (technical, financial, governance failure).
2. **Pre-coded Protocols:** Smart contract logic for treasury distribution, pausing functions, and "sunset" triggers.
3. **Communication Plans:** Public announcements, user guides, and ongoing support.
4. **Legal and Regulatory Compliance:** Final filings, tax documents, dissolution protocols.
5. **Data Export and Preservation:** Tools for user history, backups, and code release.
6. **Human Support:** Help desks, FAQs, live outreach—even after closure.

Industry Spotlight:
A Hong Kong-based DAO enshrined a "living will" in its governance—ratified by token holders, published on-chain, and updated yearly. When winding down became necessary, the transition was smooth, and users rallied behind the founders' next venture.

XIII. Tokenized Real Estate: Community-First Exit

When shelter is at stake, failure planning becomes a matter of justice.

- **Community votes** on sale, liquidation, or transfer of property.
- **Tenant protections** encoded in contracts. No eviction without cause, notification periods, and relocation support.
- **Transition to local or nonprofit management** if the protocol fails.

Global Perspective

In South Africa, real estate DAOs partner with local governments to ensure that, in failure, affordable housing is preserved and tenants are not displaced. In Canada, blockchain cooperatives transition assets to credit unions during wind-down, safeguarding both property and community.

XIV. Conclusion: The True Measure of a Project

The startup world worships launch. But the truest measure of a project is found at its end, when things go wrong, and the test of character begins. In blockchain, exit is not just an afterthought; it is the final act of stewardship.

Innovation without exit planning is not just risky, but also irresponsible. Code that can deploy must also be able to unwind. Communities that can form must also be able to grieve, preserve, and rebuild.

This chapter is a call for **maturity** for foresight. For a new, global standard in blockchain where every launch includes a final chapter already written, not because we expect to fail, but because we respect everyone involved if we do. The protocols, platforms, and founders who lead the way will not only survive the next cycle; they will be the ones who define what comes after.

The true test is not how we perform at our peak, but how we behave when it ends.

Chapter 10: The Global Convergence: Building a Universal Blockchain Ethics Standard

Summary

The blockchain revolution is no longer an experiment. It is a global transformation—one that transcends borders, legal systems, cultures, and economic strata. Yet despite its reach, the ecosystem remains fragmented. Ethical standards are inconsistent. Legal frameworks clash. Trust varies wildly across jurisdictions and communities.

Now, more than ever, we need a **universal ethics framework**—not imposed but adopted. Not enforced but embraced. A living standard that balances decentralization with duty, freedom with fairness, and code with conscience.

This final chapter lays the groundwork for global convergence. It argues not only that ethical standards are necessary, but that they are inevitable. And the time to build them is now.

The Crisis of Fragmentation

Today's Web3 landscape suffers from ethical inconsistency:

- A protocol may be fully compliant in Singapore, but banned in the U.S.
- A real estate token may protect tenant rights in one jurisdiction, but not another.
- Privacy standards vary wildly across DeFi tools.
- Token distribution practices range from radically fair to deeply predatory.

This fragmentation erodes credibility, enables exploitation, and stalls institutional trust.

What we lack is a cross-border ethical language: a shared compass for innovation.

Precedents for Ethical Convergence

History offers blueprints for global ethics:

- The Geneva Conventions for wartime conduct.
- The OECD Guidelines for multinational business behavior.
- The UN Universal Declaration of Human Rights.
- The Basel Accords for international banking risk.

Blockchain deserves its own charter—one rooted in transparency, sovereignty, and inclusive wealth-building.

We propose the **Global Code of Blockchain Ethics (G.C.B.E.)**, detailed in this book's appendix.

What the G.C.B.E. Must Include

1. **User Protections**
    - Clear disclosures, fair access, and consent-based design.
    - Right to exit, privacy by default, and redress for harm.
2. **Builder Responsibilities**
    - Transparent tokenomics, sustainability modeling, open-source audits.
    - Governance neutrality and fail-safe design.
3. **Governance Principles**
    - Inclusive voting, reputation portability, and stakeholder diversity.
    - Anti-plutocracy and bias checks in DAO structures.
4. **Investor Integrity**
    - Prohibition of deceptive marketing, hype schemes, or engineered volatility.
    - Time-weighted voting or vesting to prevent short-termism.
5. **Legal and Environmental Alignment**
    - AML/KYC compliance with ethical data standards.
    - Carbon-aware smart contract deployment and energy use transparency.
6. **Cross-Border Protocol Interoperability**
    - Ethical bridges between jurisdictions, with support for

localized compliance layers.
- Censorship resistance balanced with user safety and contextual governance.

The Role of Multilateral Engagement

The G.C.B.E. cannot emerge from a single project or nation. It must be shaped by:

- **Regulators** (e.g., SEC, ESMA, MAS)
- **Technologists and researchers**
- **Civic society and human rights advocates**
- **Developers, DAOs, and decentralized protocol leads**
- **End users, especially those from historically marginalized communities**

It is a *decentralized consensus on ethics*—built not by fiat, but by participation.

Toward Certification and Trust Marks

Once the G.C.B.E. gains adoption, ethical certification will follow:

- "Ethically Aligned Protocol" badges.
- Voluntary code audits for ethics, not just security.
- Investor disclosures tied to ethical ratings.
- Exchanges and marketplaces that reward adherence with preferential listings.

Just as organic food, LEED buildings, and B Corps created market distinctions through ethics, so too will blockchain.

Ethics becomes a trust layer—visible, provable, and valuable.

The Moral Opportunity of Blockchain

For the first time in history, we have the chance to build an economic infrastructure **not inherited, but invented**. We can choose values over legacy, ethics over convenience, and collective elevation over individual greed.

Blockchain is not just software. It is **social code**. It programs human relationships at scale. With that power comes a rare opportunity:

- To restore trust where institutions failed.
- To include those long excluded from ownership.
- To build transparency into systems—not as a requirement, but as a default.
- To create wealth without sacrificing justice.

Conclusion: The World Is Watching—Let's Lead

This book began as a blueprint, but it ends as a call to leadership.

To the developers: build with conscience.
To the investors: demand ethics.
To the regulators: regulate with nuance, not fear.
To the users: your participation is your power.

We can create a global blockchain economy that doesn't just work, but works *for everyone.*

That begins with a code—not just of logic, but of ethics.

Let this be that code.

Chapter 10: Expansion

I. Introduction: The Era of Global Blockchain

Blockchain has crossed the Rubicon. What began as a cypherpunk experiment—an attempt to code trust and minimize institutional overreach—has evolved into a global phenomenon, influencing financial markets, real estate, health, energy, governance, and the very infrastructure of the internet. Blockchains now process trillions in value, tokenize homes from Lagos to London, manage logistics in Asia, anchor elections in Latin America, and give digital identity to the unbanked in rural India.

Yet with this reach comes a stark challenge: **Fragmentation**.

The ethical standards, legal frameworks, and social expectations around blockchain remain as fractured as the protocols themselves. What is celebrated as "disruption" in Silicon Valley is banned as "instability" in Beijing. A token celebrated for transparency in Zurich is blacklisted for privacy in New York. The same protocol can enable economic liberation in Nigeria and predatory rent-seeking in New Jersey.

Without a shared moral foundation, trust in blockchain—across institutions, users, and regulators—remains fragile. The world does not merely need more technology. It needs a common language of **ethics**. The time to build that language and the infrastructure to support it is NOW.

II. The Crisis of Fragmentation: Why Standards Matter

1. Jurisdictional Disparity

A protocol may operate fully within the law in Singapore, complying with MAS (Monetary Authority of Singapore) rules, AML checks, and data protections. Yet it may find itself blacklisted by the U.S. SEC or EU ESMA. The same real estate token can be legal, even "democratizing," in Brazil or Switzerland, but run afoul of tenant protections, securities laws, or privacy regulations elsewhere.

2. Ethical Inconsistency

- Some DeFi platforms enforce rigorous KYC and privacy standards; others operate as anything-goes casinos.
- Token launches may range from radically fair, community-driven events to deeply extractive, insider-tilted cash grabs.
- DAOs experiment with governance, some championing inclusivity and deliberation, others reverting to plutocracy and insider coordination.

3. Cultural and Social Blindspots

What one culture sees as transparent and empowering, another may see as invasive or exclusionary. Privacy, wealth-sharing, property rights, and risk tolerance differ radically across continents, generations, and socioeconomic strata.

4. Institutional Distrust

Banks, asset managers, public pension funds, and governments remain hesitant. Without reliable ethical benchmarks, they cannot assess risk, reputation, or long-term viability. Fragmentation breeds skepticism.

First-Person Account:
"As a regulator, I see platforms comply with local laws, but ignore the spirit of fairness or sustainability. They arbitrage jurisdictions—moving fast in the shadows, always one step ahead. This isn't innovation. It's avoidance."
— Elena, Financial Regulator, Spain

III. Precedents for Ethical Convergence: Learning From History

Blockchain is not the first global system to face the challenge of ethical alignment across borders.

1. The Geneva Conventions

Born out of the horrors of war, the Geneva Conventions codified humane treatment across armies, nations, and ideologies. Their power came not from top-down enforcement, but from universal adoption and the recognition of shared values.

2. The OECD Guidelines

For multinational businesses, the OECD guidelines provide a moral backbone, requiring transparency, human rights protections, anti-corruption, and environmental standards, regardless of local legal loopholes.

3. The UN Universal Declaration of Human Rights

In the wake of a global catastrophe, the UN crafted a declaration that set a floor for dignity, inclusion, and justice. Today, it is invoked by citizens, NGOs, and governments worldwide, even when not legally binding.

4. The Basel Accords

Faced with global banking crises, the Basel Accords set capital and risk standards for financial institutions, enabling cross-border trust, reducing contagion, and establishing shared benchmarks for stability.

Historical Analogy:
"International banking was once as fragmented as blockchain is today.

The Basel Accords didn't erase local law, but set a floor—a standard of safety and integrity. That's what blockchain needs now."
— Jacques, Retired Central Banker, France

IV. The Case for a Global Code of Blockchain Ethics (G.C.B.E.)

The moment demands a shared framework. Not a regulatory straitjacket, but a living, adaptable code that is grounded in the realities of decentralized technology, but as ambitious as the systems it seeks to govern.

The Vision

A Global Code of Blockchain Ethics (G.C.B.E.) would provide:

- A universal language for protocols, builders, investors, users, and regulators.
- A baseline for trust, risk management, and public accountability.
- A platform for certification, market incentives, and social legitimacy.

It would not replace national laws, but harmonize ethical standards across them. It would not freeze innovation, but ensure innovation is **worthy of trust**.

V. What the G.C.B.E. Must Include: Framework and Principles

The proposed framework, detailed in this book's appendix, must be both **comprehensive** and **practical**. Here, we summarize its critical elements.

1. User Protections

- **Clear disclosures** of all risks, rewards, and rights in plain language.
- **Fair access** to participation, not gated by wealth, geography, or technical know-how.
- **Consent-based design**. Users control their data, identity, and exposure.

- **Right to exit**. Liquidity and off-ramps for tokens and investments.
- **Privacy by default**, with user-driven transparency.
- **Redress for harm**. Mechanisms for dispute resolution, restitution, and appeals.

2. Builder Responsibilities

- **Transparent tokenomics**: No hidden emissions, inflation, or privileged access.
- **Sustainability modeling**: Economic and environmental.
- **Open-source audits**: Aiming for security and ethics, not just code.
- **Governance neutrality**: Builders as facilitators, not dictators.
- **Fail-safe design**: Pre-coded wind-downs, emergency shutdowns, and user protections.

3. Governance Principles

- **Inclusive voting**: Accessible across languages, abilities, and devices.
- **Reputation portability:** Users are more than a single wallet or score.
- **Stakeholder diversity**: Multi-constituency governance.
- **Anti-plutocracy**: Checks against whale dominance, vote buying, and insider capture.
- **Bias checks**: Periodic audit of outcomes for unintended discrimination or exclusion.

4. Investor Integrity

- **Prohibition of deceptive marketing**. No engineered FOMO, no hype schemes.
- **No engineered volatility** for profit at users' expense.
- **Time-weighted voting and vesting**. Discouraging pump-and-dump, promoting stewardship.
- **Disclosure of all conflicts, incentives, and risks** beyond legal minimums.

5. Legal and Environmental Alignment

- **AML/KYC compliance**: Without mass surveillance or data

abuse.

- **Ethical data standards**: Decentralized identity, verifiable credentials, and user-controlled access.
- **Carbon-aware smart contracts**: Public energy use reporting, incentives for green infrastructure.

6. Cross-Border Protocol Interoperability

- **Ethical bridges**: Protocols must support localized compliance, but maintain user protections and ethical standards.
- **Censorship resistance balanced with safety**: Clear escalation paths for malicious content or abuse.
- **Contextual governance**: Local voices represented in protocol decision-making.

VI. The Role of Multilateral Engagement: Building Consensus

No single company, country, or chain can define global ethics. The G.C.B.E. must emerge from a **multilateral, participatory process**.

1. Stakeholder Mapping

- **Regulators** (SEC, ESMA, MAS, FATF, central banks)
- **Technologists and researchers** (blockchain developers, cybersecurity experts, academic centers)
- **Civic society and human rights advocates** (NGOs, legal aid, digital rights organizations)
- **DAOs and decentralized protocol leaders**
- **End users**, especially marginalized and at-risk communities

2. The Process

- **Open consultation**: Workshops, online fora, public comment.
- **Iterative drafting:** Versions published, debated, and amended.
- **Regional adaptation**: Local supplements for unique legal or social requirements.
- **Annual review and update**: A living standard, not a fixed doctrine.

3. The Role of Leadership

Ethical convergence is not top-down. True change comes when global leaders, respected protocols, and visionary DAOs voluntarily adopt the code—setting a market standard that others must match or surpass.

First-Person Account:
"Our DAO adopted a community-drafted ethics charter. It didn't solve every problem, but it raised the bar—and soon, other projects began to follow."
— Samuel, DAO Steward, Nigeria

VII. Toward Certification and Trust Marks: Ethics as a Market Advantage

1. "Ethically Aligned Protocol" Badges

Once the G.C.B.E. gains traction, third-party bodies or DAOs will certify protocols for alignment. Projects that meet the standard will earn visible "Ethics Verified" trust marks that will be displayed on platforms, exchanges, and dApps.

2. Voluntary Audits

Audits will go beyond code security to assess:

- User protections and consent
- Tokenomics and economic sustainability
- Governance inclusion and diversity
- Environmental impact and carbon reporting

3. Investor and User Disclosures

Projects certified under the G.C.B.E. will disclose not only technical risks, but also their ethical rating, audit history, and any outstanding compliance or social issues.

4. Market Incentives

- **Exchanges** may prioritize or even restrict listings to protocols with certified ethical alignment.

- **Funds** and institutional investors will mandate G.C.B.E. certification as a condition for capital.
- **DAOs** and communities will coalesce around projects with proven ethical DNA, creating a new layer of self-governance.

Historical Analogy:
"Organic food was once a niche. LEED buildings were for the avant-garde. B Corps were unknown. Now, all are market leaders—because ethics became a value."
— Taryn, Sustainability Fund Manager, South Africa

VIII. Sector Spotlights: Applying the G.C.B.E. Across Domains

A. Real Estate Tokenization

- Tenants' rights encoded in governance
- Transparency in property ownership and management
- Fair exit and wind-down protocols
- Community voice in land use and redevelopment decisions

B. DeFi Protocols

- Yield transparency. Returns tied to real economic activity, not Ponzi dynamics
- Access for underserved populations
- On-chain dispute resolution and fair appeals

C. Digital Identity

- Self-sovereign identities with user control over disclosure and consent
- Verifiable credentials for KYC/AML without data centralization
- Privacy by default. No blanket surveillance or lifetime blacklisting

D. Environmental Impact

- Public reporting of energy consumption
- Incentives for proof-of-stake or carbon-neutral operations
- Integration with UN Sustainable Development Goals

E. Governance and DAOs

- Quadratic or reputation-based voting
- Stakeholder diversity and bias audits
- Human-readable constitutions, with clear rights and remedies

---

IX. First-Person Perspectives: The Global Conversation

Amara, Student and DAO Member, Kenya:
"Blockchain gave me my first bank account. But I worry about fairness. A universal code means I can trust new platforms, even when they're based far away."

Hans, Regulator, Germany:
"Our greatest challenge is coordination. If the G.C.B.E. succeeds, we can harmonize rules, reduce risk, and open the door for broader adoption."

Vivian, Tech Entrepreneur, Brazil:
"Ethics as a trust badge? It would change how we raise capital, how we recruit, and how we scale. Investors and users want this—even if they don't say it directly."

Lian, Privacy Advocate, Singapore:
"Privacy is a baseline, not a luxury. Any ethics code that ignores this is incomplete. We need global pressure to keep this right alive in the next generation of the internet."

X. Barriers to Convergence: Challenges and Countercurrents

1. Regulatory Competition

Nations may hesitate to adopt standards perceived as a threat to sovereignty or local innovation.

2. Race to the Bottom

Without a global consensus, some jurisdictions may lower ethical standards to attract capital, mirroring past "offshore" races in banking, gambling, or data hosting.

3. Cultural Relativism

Universalism may clash with cultural specificity. Ethics codes must be adaptive, not imperial.

4. Technological Change

Rapid evolution may outpace standard-setting. The G.C.B.E. must be modular, upgradeable, and supported by a global community of stewards.

XI. The Moral Opportunity of Blockchain: A New Social Contract

For the first time in history, we can build not only new technology, but new norms. Blockchain is not just software; it is a social code, a programmable foundation for global economic and social relationships.

- **Restoring trust** by making transparency, not opacity, the default.
- **Including the excluded** by democratizing access, ownership, and voice.
- **Weaving justice into markets** by embedding fairness, not just efficiency, into every contract.
- **Sustaining the planet** by aligning digital economies with the realities of environmental stewardship.

First-Person Reflection:
"My parents taught me to question authority. Blockchain lets me question and build at the same time. But without shared ethics, we just reinvent the old injustices faster. This is our chance to do better."
— Rohan, Developer, India

XII. Conclusion: Leadership, Participation, and the Next Chapter

This book began as a blueprint, but it ends as a **call to leadership**. The infrastructure we build now will become the rules by which billions live, work, create, and own.

- To the **developers**: Every line of code is a moral act. Build with conscience.
- To the **investors**: Demand not just returns, but ethics. Reward the protocols that align with your values, not just your wallet.
- To the **regulators**: Lead with nuance. Regulation is not censorship; it is the architecture of trust. Join the conversation, don't just enforce from afar.
- To the **users**: You are not passive. Participation is power. Vote, speak, build. Your choices set the tone for the entire ecosystem.

The **world is watching**. This is the moment to define not just what blockchain *can* do, but what it *should* do. A universal ethics standard is not a constraint, but the very thing that will unlock blockchain's true potential—for everyone.

Let this be the code—not just of logic, but of ethics.

Let us converge—not by force, but by shared conviction.

Let us build the world's first truly global, ethical infrastructure—for finance, for property, for identity, and for the future.

Bonus Chapter

Beyond the Code – Blockchain's Invitation to a New Civilization

---

I. Prologue: The Fork in Humanity

The world is at a fork. It is not merely a question of which digital ledger will dominate, or which protocol will win the next bull market. It is the recognition that *technology is no longer just a tool for human civilization; it is the architecture of the civilization itself.* We have reached the moment when our systems do not just serve us; they shape us.

Blockchains, smart contracts, and DAOs are more than lines of code; they are scaffolds for new societies, economies, and even new moralities.

Yet, as we stand on the edge of this new era, the question is not simply what we *can* build, but what we *should* become.

II. The Mirror of Code: What Blockchain Reveals About Us

Every technological revolution holds up a mirror to the human condition.

The industrial age showed us our appetite for mastery and exploitation.

The internet revealed our hunger for connection and our struggle with truth.

Blockchain, with its promise of decentralized consensus and immutable trust, holds up a sharper mirror than ever before.

- *Who do we trust when trust itself is digitized?*
- *What becomes of authority when anyone can vote?*
- *How do we define ownership when property is just a string of numbers?*
- *What is justice when the law is written in algorithms, not statutes?*

These are not technical questions; they are existential. The answers will shape not only the future of finance and governance, but the story of our species.

III. The Three Pillars: Power, Identity, and Belonging

To understand the world blockchain is building, we must confront three fundamental questions:

1. Power: Who Decides?

For centuries, power was vertical, held by monarchs, priests, politicians, and corporations. Blockchain proposes a new geometry: horizontal, peer-to-peer, with no privileged center. This is radical, but it is also fragile. Distributed power, without ethics and oversight, can fragment into mob rule, plutocracy, or digital oligarchy.

2. Identity: Who Belongs?

Blockchains promise universal access, but identity remains fraught. Are we the sum of our wallets and transactions? Or do we still possess the dignity of self-definition, the right to start again, to be more than a string of data points? As digital identity becomes both currency and passport, we must decide: Does technology include or exclude? Does it remember our humanity, or reduce us to metadata?

3. Belonging: What Holds Us Together?

Decentralization can erode traditional anchors, including nations, communities, and even families. In their place, new tribes emerge: token holders, NFT collectors, DAOs. These bonds are powerful, but can also be brittle. Without a shared moral vision, decentralization risks becoming just another engine of division.

IV. The Paradox of Liberation and Control

Blockchain was born as a rebellion against central banks, surveillance capitalism, and institutional failure. But history teaches that every tool of liberation can become a tool of control.

- **Transparency** promises accountability, but can enable surveillance and persecution.
- **Smart contracts** automate trust, but can ossify injustice.
- **Immutable ledgers** ensure honesty, but may also entrench mistakes and punish the vulnerable.

In every age, the most dangerous myths are those that go unexamined. The myth of "neutral code" is no exception. Code is never neutral. It encodes the values, fears, and aspirations of its creators. The challenge for this generation is to make that encoding explicit, conscious, and just.

V. Voices from the Edge: Global Testimonies

A. The Politician

"I sit in parliament, watching debates rage about digital assets, and I see the gap—not of policy, but of imagination. Blockchain terrifies regulators because it makes control impossible, but excites the public because it promises fairness. My greatest fear is that we will legislate from anxiety, not vision."
— Maria, Minister of Digital Affairs, Argentina

B. The Developer

"We built our protocol to be unkillable. Then we realized—we had no idea how to fix it when things went wrong. The code had outpaced our wisdom. Now I see my job not as building faster, but building with conscience."
— Tomo, Blockchain Engineer, Japan

C. The Citizen

"For years, my family was excluded from banking. With blockchain, I can finally own something. But it's overwhelming—so much noise, so little trust. I want more than a wallet; I want a future I can believe in."
— Keisha, Community Organizer, Nigeria

VI. Political Will and the Architecture of Trust

1. Rethinking Regulation

The instinct of the state is to regulate what it cannot control, ban what it cannot understand, and punish what it cannot tax. But the politics of fear will not stop the blockchain tide; it will only drive it underground. True leadership lies in collaboration: bringing developers, citizens, and regulators to the same table, not to stifle, but to shape the future.

Industry Example:
Singapore's regulatory sandbox has allowed dozens of blockchain pilots, balancing consumer protection with innovation, fostering an environment where failure is survivable and success is scalable.

2. The Politics of Inclusion

No ethical blockchain future is possible without radical inclusion. This means not just open APIs, but active outreach: education in rural schools, onboarding for the elderly, accessibility for the disabled, and support for the digitally excluded.

First-Person Account:
"I led a DAO workshop for women in a Nairobi slum. Their first question wasn't about yield—it was about safety. Can this technology protect me, or will it just make me more visible to those who want to harm me?"
— Lillian, Digital Literacy Advocate, Kenya

VII. Developer Responsibility: Coding for Civilization

1. The Weight of Code

Developers are now lawmakers, wielding power once reserved for parliaments. Every commit to a smart contract is a micro-legislation. Every design pattern is a constitution. The ethical burden is immense.

2. The Ethics of Algorithmic Justice

Who gets to vote? How are forks resolved? What is the appeal process? The answers to these questions are encoded in the hearts of those who write the code and not just in governance tokens.

3. Collaboration Across Silos

Ethical innovation will require cross-disciplinary teams: ethicists, social scientists, legal scholars, artists, and community organizers. The future will not be written by coders alone, but by polyglot teams that understand both machine and human.

VIII. Citizens as Stewards: Participation Beyond Speculation

1. From Speculators to Stakeholders

The tragedy of blockchain's early years is the reduction of citizenship to speculation. The next chapter must revive the lost arts of stewardship and participation.

2. Building Social Capital

DAOs, identity protocols, and community platforms must reward not just financial risk, but mentorship, education, and care. Reputation systems must account for kindness as well as cleverness.

3. The New Social Contract

As people become not just users, but co-owners and co-creators, the very notion of citizenship is reborn—one wallet, one voice, but also one responsibility to the collective.

IX. Case Studies: Blockchain's Double-Edged Sword

1. The Promise and Peril of Tokenized Land in the Global South

In Brazil, tokenized land registries are helping Indigenous communities reclaim ancestral rights, but in parts of Africa, "land rush" protocols risk a new wave of digital colonization.

The lesson: Technology is only as good as its stewards.

2. Real-World Impact: Universal Basic Income

Experiments in blockchain-based Universal Basic Income (UBI) are underway in Spain, Kenya, and California. Some succeed, distributing value without middlemen. Others are gamed by whales and bots.

The difference? Governance, oversight, and ethics.

3. When DAOs Go to War

In the first DAO-vs-DAO lawsuit, two digital communities in the U.S. clashed over the ownership of a trademark. The absence of legal frameworks led to chaos, lost value, and a cautionary tale about the limits of code without consensus.

X. The World's Challenge: Choosing the Next Operating System

1. The Collapse of Old Myths

- That growth equals good.
- That technology is destiny.
- That code is law, and law is enough.

The old stories are ending. The world is choosing its next operating system, not just for finance, but for culture, identity, and governance.

2. The Emergence of New Myths

- That inclusivity is possible, even at scale.
- That justice can be programmable, but never automatic.
- That prosperity can be decoupled from extraction.

XI. The Role of Imagination: Art, Literature, and the Narrative of the Possible

Artists, writers, filmmakers, and philosophers must join the blockchain debate. Their work shapes our sense of what is possible, what is desirable, and what is dangerous.

- **Art DAOs** are redefining collective creation.
- **NFT collectives** fund social movements, not just speculative art.
- **Literature** frames the stories we tell about power, freedom, and

belonging.

First-Person Perspective:
"As a poet, I joined an NFT community not for profit, but for connection. For the first time, my work funds itself—and my audience is my collaborator."
— Omar, Digital Poet, Lebanon

XII. The Danger of Complacency: The Dystopian Fork

There are two futures ahead.

1. The Closed World

A future where blockchains become just another tool of surveillance, inequality, and exclusion. Where DAOs are captured by whales, privacy is a privilege, and digital redlining is invisible but absolute.

2. The Open World

A future where blockchain becomes the architecture of trust, the engine of inclusion, and the ground for new forms of solidarity.

The choice is not inevitable. It is a matter of will.

XIII. Building the Future: Practical Recommendations for All

For Politicians

- Listen before you legislate. Technology is not your enemy; it is your inheritance.
- Build regulatory sandboxes, not fences.
- Appoint digital ombudsmen, not just tech czars.

For Developers

- Ship slow, not just fast. Audit, debate, and iterate.
- Invite non-coders to your table. Test with the marginalized, not just the early adopters.
- Document failure just like success.

For Citizens

- Demand transparency from platforms, not just returns.
- Use your vote, your reputation, your attention as levers for good.
- Practice mutual aid and help the next user onboard, learn, and thrive.

XIV. The Blockchain Renaissance: Bridging the Chasm

We are living through a renaissance, not just in technology, but in imagination. What was once the preserve of kings and captains of industry is now programmable by the masses. But a renaissance is not guaranteed. It can become an inquisition just as easily as an enlightenment.

1. Learning from the Past

Every great transformation comes with backlash, disillusionment, and capture. The internet was meant to democratize information, but it also centralized power in a handful of platforms. Blockchain can break that cycle, but only if we remain vigilant.

2. The Global Commons

Blockchains are global by design. They require a new "commons," spaces for dialogue, conflict, experimentation, and repair.

3. Intergenerational Perspective

The decisions we make now will outlast us. Tokens, ledgers, and protocols may be immortal in ways we are not. We must think beyond quarters, cycles, and hype, toward centuries.

XV. Conclusion: The Invitation

This is not a conclusion, but an invitation—a call to every reader, whether politician, developer, or citizen. Blockchain is not destiny. It is designed. Its ethics, governance, and culture are not inherited, but invented, negotiated, and revised—by YOU.

We have the rare chance to build not just better apps, but a better world. To restore trust where it was broken. To widen participation. To encode justice, humility, and hope in the operating system of tomorrow.

The fork is before us. The eyes of history—and the hearts of generations yet unborn—are watching.

Will we code for power or for purpose?

For exclusion or inclusion?

For surveillance or for safety?

For greed or for dignity?

The choice is ours. And it begins, not with code, but with courage.

Appendix: Global Code of Blockchain Ethics (G.C.B.E.) Preamble

We, the undersigned builders, investors, regulators, and participants in the decentralized economy, recognize our collective responsibility to ensure that blockchain technologies serve the public good, respect human dignity, and promote fair, inclusive, and sustainable systems.

This Code is a living framework, a voluntary, principle-based guide for ethical conduct in blockchain design, deployment, and governance.

Section I: User Rights & Protections

Right to Transparency

All users shall have access to clear, honest, and accessible information about platform function, tokenomics, governance, risks, and rights.

Right to Privacy

Users shall retain control over their identity, transaction history, and personal data through privacy-preserving technologies and consent-based disclosures.

Right to Exit

Platforms must provide users with fair and accessible mechanisms to exit or liquidate positions without coercive penalties.

Right to Remedy

Protocols shall include mechanisms for dispute resolution, fund recovery, and harm mitigation wherever technically and legally possible.

Section II: Developer & Founder Responsibilities

Duty of Clarity

Project teams must publish token supply mechanics, vesting schedules, yield sources, and governance processes in comprehensible formats.

Duty of Sustainability

Systems must be designed for economic longevity, avoiding unsustainable emissions, yield schemes, or reliance on perpetual user inflows.

Duty of Access

Platforms must strive to accommodate non-technical users, diverse languages, and bandwidth limitations in the interface and documentation design.

Duty of Exit Planning

Developers shall include ethical wind-down, liquidation, and treasury continuity plans at the time of protocol launch.

Section III: Governance & Voting Integrity

Inclusive Governance

Voting systems must promote equitable participation, using safeguards against plutocracy (e.g., quadratic voting, time-based weighting).

Transparent Decision-Making

Proposals, votes, and governance discussions must be publicly visible, timestamped, and auditable.

Stakeholder Representation

Protocols affecting public goods (e.g., housing, infrastructure) must involve relevant community or regulatory input in governance.

Section IV: Tokenization & Financial Ethics

Fair Token Distribution

Tokens shall not be disproportionately allocated to insiders, early-stage capital, or privileged parties without clear disclosure and justification.

Ethical Yield Practices

Projects must disclose whether token rewards are backed by real economic activity or dependent on user inflows (Ponzi).

Mechanics are prohibited.

Real-Asset Tokenization Principles

Real estate or infrastructure tokenization must include tenant protections, property stewardship standards, and safeguards against speculative abuse.

Section V: Compliance, Regulation & Law

Proactive Compliance

Platforms must align with applicable securities, AML, tax, and consumer protection laws while advocating for clear, modern regulatory frameworks.

Ethical KYC & Data Collection

Identity verification must prioritize minimal disclosure, self-sovereign identity frameworks, and decentralized data custody where possible.

Cross-Jurisdictional Accountability

International protocols must assess the ethical implications of offering services in jurisdictions with conflicting rights, protections, or risks.

Section VI: Environmental and Social Sustainability

Carbon Responsibility

Protocols shall measure and disclose the environmental footprint of consensus mechanisms and commit to sustainable practices.

Societal Impact Review

Tokenized systems that affect labor, land, or community structures must include impact assessments and equity-based design considerations.

Section VII: Ethical Failures and Wind-Downs

Graceful Exit Protocols

Smart contracts must include treasury redistribution logic, sunset paths, and dispute-resolution mechanisms in case of failure.

Founder Accountability

Team members must not engage in insider withdrawals, unauthorized fund transfers, or abandonment during active failure conditions.

Section VIII: Certification, Enforcement & Evolution

Voluntary Adoption and Certification

Projects may self-certify or pursue third-party ethics audits to display compliance with the G.C.B.E., including badges, registry listings, and public pledges.

Open Governance of this Code

The G.C.B.E. shall be maintained by a decentralized ethics council representing diverse stakeholder groups and geographies.

Periodic Review

This Code shall be revised annually to account for emerging technologies, use cases, and societal impact factors.

Final Clause: The Ethical Future Is Now

This Code is not law, nor is it perfect. But it is a step toward responsible freedom, where trust is earned through transparency, power is checked by principle, and innovation serves humanity.

We invite you—whether builder, regulator, investor, or participant—to sign, implement, and evolve this code as part of the ethical foundation for a truly decentralized world.

* 9 7 9 8 9 9 3 0 8 2 5 8 5 *
SD - #0048 - 140926 - C0 - 229/152/9 - PB - 9798993082585 - Gloss Lamination